THE HUNTER'S SHOOTING GUIDE

RIFLES • SHOTGUNS • HANDGUNS

Jack O'Connor

OUTDOOR LIFE BOOKS
New York

STACKPOLE BOOKS
Harrisburg, Pennsylvania

Originally published under the title *Outdoor Life Shooting Book*, now completely revised and updated.

Copyright © 1957, 1978 by Jack O'Connor

Published by
Outdoor Life Books
Times Mirror Magazines, Inc.
380 Madison Avenue
New York, NY 10017

Distributed to the trade by
Stackpole Books
Box 1831
Cameron & Kelker Streets
Harrisburg, PA 17105

Library of Congress Catalog Card Number: 57-5180
ISBN: 0-943822-00-9

First Edition, 1957
Second Edition, Revised and Updated, 1978

Ninth Printing, 1984

Manufactured in the United States of America

Preface

to the new edition
by Jim Carmichel

With the possible exception of Theodore Roosevelt, no man of this century has had a greater impact on hunting and sport shooting than Jack O'Connor. His hunting adventures, his observations of the hunting scene, and his ability to describe them in a style uniquely his own made him the most listened-to sportsman-writer in America for nearly two generations.

At the time of his death at seventy-six he was as prolific as ever and his rapier sharp observations had lost none of their keenness. In this, his last major writing effort, Jack O'Connor shows us one more time that in addition to being one of the world's great shooting and hunting authorities he was also one of the great artists of the English language.

When he speculates he says so but this seldom occurs because his advice is based on one of the greatest lifelong hunting experiences of all time. His analysis of firearms performance is unfailingly just, original and laced through and through with common sense. He pulls no punches and keeps no secrets.

To inform and instruct in a clear, concise manner requires great talent, but to entertain as well takes genius. No one could do it better than O'Connor, as readers of this book will quickly discover.

Contents

Types of Rifle Actions

AT ONE TIME a great many rifles were made on various types of single-shot actions. Most of them were of the falling-block type, and they were made in all calibers from the little .22 short to big .45/100 Sharps for long-range buffalo shooting. Widely used actions were the Stevens No. 44 and 44$^1/_2$, the Winchester Model 1879, the Sharps and Sharps-Borchardt, the British Farquharson, the Remington Hepburn. A somewhat different single-shot action was the Remington rolling block, which was a favorite for military use all over the world and which is seen on thousands of old military rifles, some in calibers as modern as the 7mm Mauser.

The heyday of the single-shots came in the last third of the nineteenth century before the development of repeating actions that would handle large powerful cartridges for the largest game. The buffalo hunters used single-shot Sharps, Sharps-Borchardt, and Remington rifles for long, straight-taper, rimmed black-powder cartridges of from .38 to .50 caliber. The British used various single-shots, among them the excellent Farquharson for powerful black-powder cartridges and later for smokeless-powder cartridges. Actually, many of the "Nitro Express" cartridges until recently made in England were simply the old black-powder jobs loaded with smokeless powder and jacketed bullets.

Hunters found the repeating action much superior to single-shots for practical uses. A second and third shot could be fired quickly and there was no fumbling to reload as often happens with single-shots. Then as pressures went higher with smokeless powder, single-shot actions gave extraction trouble with early brass cartridge cases, as these tended to be soft.

For the "hotter" large-caliber smokeless-powder cartridges the British went to Mauser and Magnum Mauser bolt actions. Americans developed actions capable of handling powerful cartridges. Among these were the Model 1876 and Model 1886 Winchester lever actions and the Winchester Model 1895. These actions could handle cartridges like the .33 Winchester and the .45/70 in the Model 1886 and the .38/72 (black-powder) and the .35 Winchester and .405 Winchester (smokeless) in Winchester Model 95.

Winchester made its good, Browning-designed Model 1885 single-shot in calibers from .22 to .405 and even in some shotgun gauges, but it was later discontinued. From then on for a good many years single-shots were seen only on "kids'" .22s like the Stevens Crack Shot and inexpensive .22s which locked only by the bolt handle turning into a slot in the receiver. During this time gun lovers shopped around for old single-shot actions like the Winchester Model 95, the Remington Hepburn, and the Stevens No. 44$\frac{1}{2}$ and had them barreled to hot varmint calibers, usually .22s.

But in recent years the single-shot has undergone a revival. Ruger brought out the Number One single-shot based more or less on the old Farquharson action much improved. It is chambered for a great variety of cartridges from the .243 to the .458.

The Ruger Number One single-shot. This is the Tropical Rifle, for .375 H & H Magnum or .458 Winchester Magnum, but the Number One is available in a great variety of calibers. Note the simplicity and ruggedness of the action.

For some types of hunting the single-shot makes sense. A Ruger Number One with a 24-inch barrel, for example, has the same overall length as a bolt-action rifle with a 24-inch barrel. Such a rifle in 7 x 57, .270, .280, or .30/06 would make a dandy sheep rifle. Sheep are usually killed with one shot, and a short, light rifle is easier to carry around in rough country than a heavier one. Browning also has reintroduced the old single-shot that Browning called the Model 1879 and Winchester the Model 1885. Colt made a single-shot very briefly but decided it could not be marketed profitably. Two or three good single-shot actions made largely by hand are available from custom gunsmiths.

The Ruger Number Three, a carbine, has the same action as the Number One but a different-style lever.

In the early days of smokeless powder, many big-game rifles were built on single-shot actions just as they were for black-powder big-game cartridges in the days of the buffalo slaughter in the 1870s and 1880s. However, as the various repeating actions were perfected fewer and fewer single shots were used on big game.

THE LEVER-ACTIONS

At one time the overwhelming favorite for big-game hunting in the United States was the lever-action repeater with tubular magazine, and it is still extremely popular. The Spencer and Henry carbines of the Civil War period were lever-actions, and the famous old Winchester Models 73 and 76 were likewise of this type. The best seller of all time in the way of a big game rifle is the Winchester Model 94. Over 4,500,000 of the model have been made. It is still being manufactured in the form of the Model 94 carbine and in the slightly different "commemorative" models. The Winchester Model 71 for the .348 cartridge was a modernized version of the old Winchester Model 1886, and like the Model 94 it employed a tubular magazine.

The Marlin lever-action big-game rifles are in general similar to the Winchester Model 94 rifles and they employ the same tubular magazine. They include the Model 336, available in .30/30 and, for the 336C, .35 Remington; the Model 1894, in .44 Remington Magnum; the Model 1895, in .45/70; and the Model 444, in, obviously, .444 Marlin. Unlike the Winchesters they eject their fired cases to the side instead of straight up and are hence more suitable for mounting scopes as they can be put on low and central over the bore. Scopes put on Winchester Model 94 rifles must be offset.

Winchester lever-actions. From top to bottom, the Model 94 (this one a "Limited Edition 1977" costing $1,500), the Model 1895, and the Model 88. The M94 is still going strong but the others are obsolete.

Great advantages of the Winchester and Marlin lever-action rifles are the speed of fire and the ease of learning to operate the lever fast, and also the ability to insert cartridges in the magazine without opening the action. One disadvantage is that in tubular magazines sharp-pointed bullets cannot be used without the danger of firing a cartridge by recoil, since the sharp point would rest on the primer of the cartridge ahead. The fact that these actions do not lock at the head of the breechbolt and that cartridge cases stretch on firing is another. These actions lack the camming action of the Mauser-type bolt and hence are inferior in the ability to extract dirty, soft, or oversize cases. Rifles on these actions are primarily fairly light handy deer rifles for short and medium range shooting of deer, moose and bear in wooded country. Cartridges made for them are for the most part of medium power and give moderate pressures.

Marlin lever-actions. From top to bottom, the Model 336C (carbine), the Model 1894, the Model 1895, and the Model 444. The M336 is a popular .30/30.

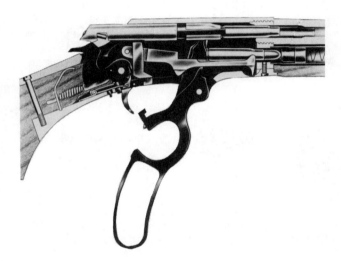

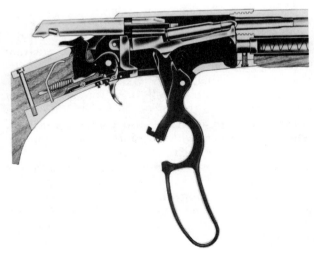

Cutaway of the Marlin M336 action just after firing, partially opened, and fully opened.

The obsolete lever-action Winchester Model 95 rifle had a stronger action than the Model 94 and was made for larger and more potent cartridges, not only for big black-powder cartridges like the .38/72 and .40/72, but for powerful smokeless-powder big-game cartridges like the .30/40, the now obsolete .35 and .405 Winchester cartridges, and the .30/06. The Model 95 had a box magazine, avoiding the problems of the tubular magazine.

Another fine lever-action suitable for cartridges giving high pressures and employing sharp-pointed bullets is the Model 99 Savage, which has been one of the favorite big-game rifles in the United States now for three-quarters of a century. The Model 99 employs a spool-type magazine similar to that used in the famous Mannlicher-Schoenauer big game rifle. The action is a very strong one as it has a massive breechbolt which wedges into a strong receiver and hence has practically no give. The Model 99 has been made in .25/35, .30/30 Winchester, .303 Savage, .22 Savage High Power, .250/3000, and .300 Savage. It is no longer made for the first four cartridges, but it is still being chambered for the last two. In addition it is made for the new high-intensity .243, .308, and .358 Winchester cartridges. Another virtue of the Model 99, besides its good magazine and strong action, is the fact that the rifle ejects cases to the side and is suitable for low scope mounting.

The Savage Model 99A has a straight-grip stock and schnabel fore-end. The M99C comes with a pistol grip. Both have a spool rather than tubular magazine and hence can take sharp-pointed bullets.

The Winchester Model 88 was one of the most interesting rifles to be designed in many years. The 88 overcomes just about all the objections that have been made to lever-action rifles. The only one that I have shot was one of the first production models in .308 W.C.F. caliber, and it was astonishingly accurate. Reason for this is that the Model 88 is simply a bolt-action operated by a lever, a rifle with just about all the advantages of each type. Like the bolt-action, the rifle has a one-piece stock that stiffens the whole assembly up and makes for better accuracy. Also like the bolt-action, the Model 88 has a breechbolt which locks with lugs at the head and hence gives the cartridge cases no chance to stretch. The operating lever has a fast, short throw, and the detachable box magazine carries the cartridges in staggered array and does away with the shortcomings of the tubular magazine. Like the Mauser-type bolt action, the Model 88 action has a cam to facilitate extraction. The Model 88 was made for the .243, the .308, and .358 W.C.F. cartridges, but in spite of its virtues it was never popular and has been dropped.

THE PUMP-ACTIONS

The pump action, also called the slide or trombone action, has been widely used for .22 repeating rifles but the only pump-action big-game rifle currently manufactured is the Remington Model 760, which is an excellent, fast-operating, nicely stocked rifle with a strong rotary breechbolt locking with multiple lugs at the head. The model 760 is primarily a woods rifle for rapid shooting. It weighs $7^1/_2$ pounds and is currently made for the .30/06, .270 W.C.F., .308, .243, and 6mm Remington. Savage now (1978) makes the model 170-C pump-action carbine in .30/30 only.

In the past, other pump-action big-game rifles have been made. One was the Remington Model 14 and its revised successor, the Model 141 for the Remington rimless line of cartridges—.25, .30, .32, and .35. An earlier Remington pump was for the low-pressure cartridges like the .38/40 and .44/40.

The Remington Model 760 is one of only two high-powered big-game pump-action rifles now made. The other is the Savage .30/30 pump.

Colt, the handgun manufacturer, at one time made the Lightning Model pump for .22 rimfire cartridges and for low-pressure varmint and big-game cartridges like the .32/20 and .44/40. An ill-starred concern called the Standard Arms Co. at one time before World War I made rifles that could be used either as gas-operated semi-automatics or pump-actions. They were chambered for the Remington rimless line of cartridges.

The principal advantage of the pump action is that next to the semi-automatic it is the fastest of all actions, and it is very easy to work from the shoulder. It is instinctively liked by men used to the popular American pump shotgun like the Winchester Model 12 and Remington Model 870. Disadvantage is lack of extracting power as compared to the bolt-action, the two piece stock, and the slide handle hung o￼ the barrel. Accuracy is good enough for woods hunting, but inferior to that of the bolt and even to that of the automatic for mountain hunting.

THE SEMI-AUTOMATICS

Possibly the ultimate in rifle actions is the semi-automatic, and surely it is the ultimate for the military rifle. The soldier often has to help turn back a charge and has a choice of many targets as fast as he can shoot. The hunter, on the other hand, seldom needs to fire many shots fast. His first shot is the most important and he never has to stop a charge of enraged bighorn rams or lesser kudu. Accuracy, ease of carrying, and handling for the sporting rifle are more important than the speed of fire.

The Remington Model 742 is the latest big-game semi-auto and comes in some useful calibers. It is also available as a carbine in .30/06 and .308 Winchester only.

The U.S. military rifle of World War II was a semi-automatic—the famous M-1 rifle or Garand chambered for the .30/06 cartridge. Many systems of operating semi-automatic rifles are used, and the Garand uses gas taken off near the muzzle to operate a long rod which in turn operates the action. The rifle with which we fought the Vietnam war was the M-16 for the hot .223 cartridge. Presumably this is the current combat rifle.

The Browning BAR semi-auto rifle, in Grade 1. It is available in .30/06, .270, .308, and .243, 7mm Remington Magnum, and .300 and .338 Winchester Magnum.

First Winchester automatic was the little Model 1903 for the .22 Winchester Autoloading cartridge. Others have been the Model 1905 for the inconsequential Winchester .32 and .35 self-loading cartridges, the Model 1907 for the .351 self-loader, and the Model 1910 for the .401 self-loading cartridge. All these Winchester rifles operated on the simple blowback principle. This makes a heavy breechblock necessary, as the breechblock is held against the case by a spring. All the Winchester self-loading cartridges look like large pistol cartridges. None of these rifles was very popular, and all are gone today.

The Remington Model 8 and the later Model 81 were self-loading or semi-automatic, if you wish, big-game rifles for the Remington rimless line of cartridges. The models differed only in their stocks and in minor refinements. Both used the long-recoil system in which the barrel and breechbolt are locked together and recoil for several inches. Then the barrel goes forward while the breechbolt is held back. The same system is used for the Remington and Browning automatic shotguns.

A semi-automatic rifle for big-game hunting and one of the best for this purpose ever built is the Remington Model 742 for the .30/06, .243, .270, and .308. This rifle is gas-operated with the gas taken off near the breech instead of near the muzzle as is the case with the Garand. It is surprisingly accurate, more so than the Model 760 pump. Harrington & Richardson also makes a fine semi-automatic, the Model 360 "Ultra Auto," available in .243 or .308 Winchester caliber.

The author shooting the Remington M742.

Some of the available .22 autoloaders. From top to bottom, the Browning Automatic .22, the Remington Model 552 BDL Deluxe, the Marlin Model 99C, the Weatherby Mark XXII, and the Ruger 10/22.

Browning's BAR is another popular autoloader, and Ruger makes an auto carbine in .44 magnum. But that's about it for center-fire semi-autos.

However, most American rifle manufacturers make semi-automatic .22 rifles. Winchester makes the Model 190, and until recently made the M290 and M490; Browning makes the BAR-22, which looks like the high-powered Browning, as well as the swag-bellied Automatic 22; Remington makes the Model 552 and the Nylon 66; Marlin makes the 42 DeLuxe, Model 99C, Model 99Ml, and Model 989M2; Weatherby makes the Mark XXII; and Ruger makes the Model 10/22. And there are others.

THE BOLT-ACTIONS

The Mauser-type bolt action is the most universally successful, most imitated, and most widely used rifle action in the world. After various experimental models were brought out in the ten years starting in 1888, the action achieved what is basically its final form with the model of 1898. Changes since then have been in the nature of refinements.

The Winchester Model 70 bolt-action. At top is a pre-1964 M70 in .375 Magnum—a real collector's item. Below it is a post-1964 M70, still a good solid rifle and available in most popular calibers.

The Mauser-type action is of the turnbolt type and has two massive locking lugs at the front end of the bolt. They turn into recesses in the receiver ring. There is a cam on the bolt to give power to extraction, and in the Model 98 and later models, there is an auxiliary locking lug at the root of the bolt. The magazine is of the box type which carries the cartridges in a staggered double column. The original Mauser action was made at Oberndorf, Germany, and in three lengths—short, for the 6.5 x 54, the 8 x 51 or 8mm—K cartridge, the .35 Remington, and .250/3000 Savage; standard for cartridges no longer than those of the 8 x 57–.30/06 class; and magnum for long cartridges like the .300 and .375 Magnums, the .404 Jeffery, and the .416 Rigby. The Mauser Werke sold actions to gunmakers all over the world, and there were many different variations of these three basic actions—in types of bridge, of floorplate release, of length and width of magazines, etc. For example, a Magnum Mauser action for the .416 Rigby cartridge would take a different magazine as well as bolt face

The Ruger Model 77 bolt-action. Round top model is shown in photo of entire gun. Detail photo shows model with male dove-tails on the receiver ring and bridge which are integral with the receiver and make for very solid scope mounting. With its classic stock lines and Mauser-type action, the whole rifle is very solid. In one version or another it's available in various calibers from .22/250 to .458 Magnum.

and extractor than the same action for the .375, and a standard action for the 8 x 60 would take a different magazine from one for the .30/06.

In addition there were variations of the Mauser action as made for military rifles, and Mauser actions have been made in Belgium, Czechoslovakia, Austria, Turkey, Iran, and Mexico as well as in Germany.

Most of the world's bolt-action rifles are simply revisions of the basic Mauser action. The famous Model 1903 Springfield used by the U.S. armed forces until the adoption of the M—1 Garand is a modified Mauser. So is the U.S. Model 1917 Enfield or British Pattern 1914, as it is also called.

The Remington Model 700 is another very solid Mauser-type bolt-action. The Classic model at top has a plain stock; the heavy-barreled BDL Varmint Special has a Monte Carlo. The M700 is also available in calibers from .222 to .458, and you can even get it in .17 Remington.

The Weatherby bolt-action line includes the Mark V, at top, which is made in all Weatherby calibers plus .22/250 and .30/06, and the less expensive Vanguard, below, which is not made in Weatherby calibers but in a good range of others from .25/06 to .300 Winchester Magnum. Both shown are fitted with Weatherby scopes.

Bolt-action rifles not of the Mauser type are the Mannlicher-Schoenauer, the Krag-Jorgenson, the obsolete Model 40 and 41 Savage big game rifles, the British Short Lee Enfield, and certain others.

Sporting-rifle actions built on Mauser principles were the Winchester Model 54 and Model 70, the Remington Model 30 and Model 720, both of which are revisions of the Model 1917 Enfield, the Remington Model 721 and Model 722, the Savage Model 1920, and the various rifles built on Mauser actions manufactured at the Fabrique Nationale concern in Belgium. The current Ruger Model 77 and Remington Model 700 actions are essentially the Model 98 Mauser, but the Weatherby and Colt-Sauer actions are changed so much they can no longer be said to be of Mauser inspiration. Mauser actions are widely used by gunsmiths.

The various bolt-action .22 rifles made by American rifle manufacturers do not incorporate Mauser principles.

The Mauser-type bolt-action rifle has many virtues—great strength, great camming power to extract the fired cartridge and to press home a fresh one, a wide extractor to grab the fired cartridge, rigidity of action that does not permit the cartridge case to stretch, a rigid barrel and action assembly which combined with a front locking bolt and a one-piece stock result in great accuracy, extreme simplicity, and great strength and ruggedness. On the other hand the bolt action is slower than other types of actions.

For those who can afford it, a very handsome custom job: an altered Mauser action in .270 by Tom Burgess, with a beautifully shaped French walnut stock by Earl Milliron. The scope is a Leupold 7.5X.

Vast numbers of little bolt-action .22s are sold annually. This typical example is the Remington Model 581, with single-shot adapter.

Because of the great strength of the bolt action, it is used mostly for high-pressure cartridges like the .270, .30/06, .300 Magnum, .458 Winchester in the United States. In Europe it is the only repeating action in use. Most of the fine magazine rifles built in England for such cartridges as the .300 H. & H., the .404, and the .416 employ Mauser actions. Since the last war some have been built on the Mauser-inspired Model 1917.

Almost all rifle enthusiasts who reload their own ammunition use bolt-action rifles. The type is being displaced for military use by the semi-automatic; but for big-game hunting it will be around for a long, long time.

The Double Rifle

A type of rifle seldom seen in the United States and dying out everywhere is the double-barrel. Actually it is two single-shot rifles, as the barrels have locks which function independently, and one of the advantages of the double rifle is that if one barrel or lock goes haywire the other can still function.

The author shooting a Holland & Holland double rifle. The idea of the double is to provide shotgun-like speed on dangerous game at close range.

Doubles have been built in Austria, Spain, Germany, and Belgium, as well as in England, but the better-known ones are mostly of British make—such famous and romantic names as Holland & Holland, Rigby, Purdey, Westley Richards. Although they have been made for a great variety of cartridges from .22 Savage High Power to .600 Nitro Express and for rimless cartridges like the .270 and .30/06 as well as for rimmed ones, most are made for powerful, rimmed big game cartridges.

On the continent many doubles in over-and-under form have been built, but in England almost all are made in conventional side-by-side form and on actions similar to those used in double-barrel shotguns.

The advantages of the double are this fact of having two rifles instead of one, the speed of the second shot, the fact of short overall length and balance between the hands with consequent quick aim and shooting, and low line of sight.

Disadvantages are the great expense (a good British double will cost from $5,000 to $15,000), the difficulty of getting the two barrels to shoot together, the cost of replacing worn-out barrels, and indifferent accuracy at the longer ranges.

But in a large caliber a good double ejector with non-automatic safety is probably the world's best life insurance.

2

How Cartridges Are Classified

THE AMERICAN GUN TRADE classifies cartridges as *rimfires, centerfire* metallics, and shot shells. The best known example of the rimfire cartridges is the common .22 and possibly 98 percent of all rimfire cartridges sold in the United States are of that caliber. However, .25 and .32 rimfire cartridges were still made and sold until fairly recently. The rimfire system of priming was the first used in fixed metallic ammunition and at one time many rimfire cartridges of large caliber were manufactured. The old .41 Swiss rimfire cartridge was on cartridge lists in the United States until about 1941, and a 9mm rimfire shotshell was discontinued a generation ago.

The centerfire system of priming is used, of course, in both rifle and pistol cartridges and shotshells, but shotshells are manufactured with brass bases and cardboard bodies. Centerfire metallics, then, are for rifles and handguns, and are, of course, so divided.

Shotshells are often spoken of as being "low-base" or "high-base." The low-base shells are made with lower brass bases and are loaded generally with comparatively mild charges of powder and light or medium charges of shot. These are the so-called trap and skeet loads and field loads for upland game. High-base shells are loaded with heavy charges of progressive-burning powder and heavy loads of shot and are intended for long-range wildfowl shooting. For many years the term "magnum" when referring to shotshells meant an extra-long and extra-powerful shell. The 12-gauge Magnum shell, for example, was always 3 inches in length and loaded with as much as $1^5/_8$ ounces of shot as compared to $1^1/_4$ in the heaviest standard $2^3/_4$-inch shell. A 3-inch 20-gauge shell is likewise made and it handles $1^3/_{16}$ ounces of shot, almost as much as the old maximum load for the $2^3/_4$-inch case in the 12-gauge.

Recently $2^3/_4$-inch Magnum shells have been manufactured, with additional powder and shot being crowded into the $2^3/_4$-in. case by reducing the wadding. The shells may be used in any good gun with $2^3/_4$-inch chambers. The 12-gauge $2^3/_4$-inch Magnum shell holds $1^1/_2$ ounces of shot. (The 3-inch Magnum has recently been stepped up to $1^7/_8$ ounces.)

When smokeless powder came into wide use in such cartridges as the .30/30, the .30/40, the .25/35, and other pioneers of a new era, they became known as "high-power" or "high-velocity" cartridges to distinguish them from their black-powder contemporaries. The velocities they turned up ran around 2,000 fps, whereas the black-powder cartridges have velocities of from 1,300 to 1,600 fps. The term "express," which is used to some extent even today, meant a black-powder big-game cartridge that had been speeded up by the use of a larger charge of black powder and a lighter bullet, usually with a hollow point. The bullet fired in "high-power" rifles moved even faster than those fired in the expresses.

In England many of the large-caliber smokeless-powder cartridges were identical to the old black-powder cartridges in exterior dimensions. They were, however, made with stronger cases and they were loaded with smokeless Cordite powder rather than black. They were then known as "nitro express" cartridges and their black-powder twins were called "b.p. expresses."

In the United States, the term "high-intensity" cartridge is sometimes used, but it has never really caught on. It came into being when such cartridges as the .30/06, the .250/3000 Savage, and the .280 Ross stepped velocities up from around 2,000 fps to 2,700–3,000 fps. In England these cartridges were called "magnums," a term borrowed, I believe, from the extra-large bottle of champagne. It simply refers to any cartridge with an extra-large case and giving high velocity. Since the first so-called "magnum" cartridges used in the United States were the belted .300 and .375 Holland & Holland Magnum cartridges from England, the term "magnum" in this country generally is applied to a cartridge with a belted case.

The British divide their cartridges into various classes according to bore. Major Sir Gerald Burrard lists five classes as follows: large bores, or rifles of calibers not less than .45 inch; heavy medium bores, less than .45 but not less than .40; medium bores, less than .40 but not less than .318; magnum medium bores, or rifles of medium caliber developing not less than 2,500 fps; small bores, rifles of calibers of less than .318; magnum small bores, or rifles with bores of less than .318 developing velocities of 2,500 fps or more; light game rifles—or any such rifle with less than 1,500 foot-pounds of energy or with a bullet of less than 50 grains.

According to the British classification, the only large-bore American factory-made rifle is the .458 Winchester. The .375 H. & H. Magnum is a medium bore, the .30/06 a magnum small bore, likewise the .270 and the .257.

In the United States the tendency is to classify cartridges as to their use. We speak of "deer cartridges," meaning those that are suitable for whitetail deer and black bear in wooded areas where ranges are not long. Typical of such cartridges are the famous .30/30 with a 170-grain bullet at 2,200 fps and the .35 Remington with a 200-grain bullet at approximately the same velocity. By "varmint cartridges" we mean those that drive light bullets of small diameter at high velocity and are intended to use on the nongame birds and animals such as woodchucks, crows, ground squirrels, and preda-

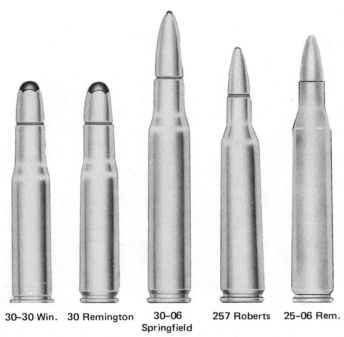

| 30–30 Win. | 30 Remington | 30–06 Springfield | 257 Roberts | 25–06 Rem. |

Left to right, the famous .30/30, so called because it is a .30 caliber with a case that has a capacity of 30 grains of black powder; the .30 Remington, ballistically similar to the .30/30 but rimless and made by Remington; the .30/06, so called because it was the U.S. military cartridge, caliber .30, Model 1906; the .257 Roberts, named for the groove diameter and the man who designed it; and the .25/06, simply a .30/06 necked down to .25.

tory hawks. Examples are the .22 Hornet, the .220 Swift, and the .244 Remington.

"All-around" cartridges are those with enough bullet weight and velocity to be used on anything from small deer to grizzly bear and moose. Examples are the .270, the .300 Magnum, and the .30/06. Of cartridges for heavy game, as heavy game is known on this continent, we have but few—the .375 Magnum, the .458, the .338, etc.

A "wildcat" cartridge is one that is not in regular factory production and distributed through the arms trade. Famous wildcats include the .22/.250 (.250/3000 Savage case necked to .22), the .35 Whelen (.30/06 case with neck expanded to .35), and .25/06 (.30/06 case necked down to .25).

HOW CARTRIDGES ARE NAMED

As is not exactly a secret, shotgun gauges are named from the number of balls of the bore diameter that it takes to weigh a pound. For example, 12 balls of the diameter of a 12-gauge bore weigh 1 pound, 16 in 16 guage, etc. Formerly guns in 4, 6, 8, 10, 12, 14, 16, 18, 20, 24, and 28 gauge were made. The 4, 6, and 8 gauges were legislated out of existence in the United States. The 10 gauge is undergoing a revival of a sort as wildfowl shooters try to reach out farther and farther. Although still made in Europe, the 14, 18 and 24 gauges are completely dead here. The 28 gauge, although a fine gauge for quail shooting, is kept alive largely by skeet shooters in the small-bore classification. The so-called .410 gauge is not a gauge at all, but a caliber, and so is the 9mm gauge which is loaded in Europe but not at this time in the United States. Of all gauges the 12 is by far the most popular, followed by the 20, 16, .410, 10, and 28 gauges in that order.

In the black-powder days rifle cartridges were generally named from their bore diameter followed by the capacity in grains of black powder and then sometimes by the bullet weight. An example would be the .45/70/500—or a .45 caliber with 70 grains of black powder driving a 500-grain bullet. Of cartridges so named still on the lists there are the .32/20, .38/40, and .44/40 among others. Smokeless-powder cartridges so named are the .30/30, .30/40, and .25/35.

Many cartridges are named from the bore diameter followed by the name of the firm that introduced them. Winchester prefers to call the .30/30 the .30 W.C.F. or .30 Winchester Center Fire, for example. The obsolete .22 W.C.F. was the .22 Winchester Center Fire, the ancestor of the .22 Hornet. More examples are the .35 Remington, the .270 Winchester, and the .303 Savage. Sometimes the name of the type of rifle it is to be fired in is included, such as a .35 Winchester Self-Loading, .30 Remington Auto, or .25/20 Repeater.

But some cartridges are named for the groove diameter of the barrel rather than the bore diameter. The .308 Winchester is simply a .30 caliber named for the groove diameter, just as the .257 is a .25 caliber. Other cartridges named for the groove diameter are the .348 W.C.F., the .375 Magnum, the .244 Remington, and the .22 Hornet.

Sometimes other odd and interesting information is added to the name. The "06" in .30/06 tells us that the cartridge was adopted in 1906 and was a .30 caliber. The "3000" in .250/3000 tells us that the original velocity of the 87-grain bullet was 3,000 f.p.s.

Of late years it has been fashionable to add an inspiring and descriptive name to calibers—.22 Hornet, .218 Bee, .219 Zipper, .220 Swift, .22 Varminter. Some of the names, such as Thunderbolt, Tornado, and so on, would make your blood run cold.

But, alas, sometimes the names of cartridges do not even come close to describing the caliber. Most .32 caliber handgun cartridges are in reality slightly oversize .30 calibers, and with few exceptions the so-called .38s are in reality .35s. The only ".38" that sails under its true colors is the .357 Magnum, which is named for the groove diameter of the barrel. The .38/40 is actually about a .39 caliber in bore diameter and a .40 caliber in groove diameter. The .44/40 is a .42 in reality and the .44 Smith & Wesson Special and .44 Magnums are more properly about .42s in bore diameter with bullet diameters of .43. Like most of our .38s, the 9mm European pistol cartridges are .35s with bullet diameters running from .354 to .356.

European practice is to name cartridges from the bore diameter of the rifle firing them in millimeters and then follow this with the case length.

The cartridges we know as 7mm and 8mm Mausers are in Europe generally called the 7 x 57 and the 7.9 or 8 x 57. The 8 x 57 was first brought out in 1888 for the Model 88 German military rifle sometimes called the 88 Mauser and sometimes the 88 Mannlicher. The bullet measured about .318 inch. This cartridge is generally known as the 8 x 57 J, as the J and I are pretty much interchangeable in German and the J stands for infantry. In 1905 the cartridge was given a lighter sharp-pointed or "spitzer" bullet of somewhat larger diameter (.323 inch). This cartridge is called the 7.92mm or the 8 x 57 JS—J for infantry and S for Spitzer. Because the Germans built many single-shots, combination guns, and double rifles that work best with rimmed cartridges, most rimless cartridges for magazine rifles have rimmed counterparts. The rimmed 7 x 57 is, of course, known as the 7 x 57 R and the rimmed counterpart of the regular 8 mm Mauser is the 8 x 57 JR.

We have always called the European cartridges by their metric names but the English, for the most part, do not. Long ago they took the 7 x 57 to their bosoms, but they have usually called it the .275 or the .276. Since many rifles were made for it by the firm of John Rigby, it is often called the .275 Rigby, and when it uses a 140-grain bullet stepped up to 2,750 fps, it becomes the .275 Rigby Magnum. The German 7 x 57-R when manufactured in England for a Holland & Holland double rifle becomes the 7mm Magnum.

Famous German cartridges used widely over the world besides the 7 x 57 and the 8 x 57 are the 7 x 64, a sort of a German .270; the 9.3 x 62, which is similar to the American wildcat .35 Whelen; and the 10.75.

Just as we load some German and British cartridges, the Germans and British load some of ours. When manufactured in Germany our .30/06 is called the 7.62 x 63, the .30/30 the 7.62 x 51, the .25/35 the 6.5 x 51, the .22 Hornet the 5.6 x 35-R. A few cartridges are used all over the world and loaded wherever cartridges are made. Among them are the .30/06, the 7mm and 8mm Mauser cartridges, and the .375 Magnum. The .270 Winchester, which is loaded in England and Sweden, and probably in Germany and Belgium, is rapidly assuming the character of an international cartridge.

Shotgun gauges are international, although of course there are minor differences in bore diameter, just as there are with guns of different make in this country. But Belgian or British 12-gauge shells will work in an American 12-gauge gun, Spanish 20-gauge shells in an American 20-gauge, and so on. Instead of using the term "gauge" the British usually speak of a "12 bore" and the continentals of a "caliber 12."

American chambers have been standardized in 12, 16, 20, and 28 gauge as $2^3/_4$ inches, except for the 12- and 20-gauge magnums and the .410, which are 3 inches long. However, most British shotguns were chambered for $2^1/_2$-inch shells and so are most continental guns. It is usually mandatory for a British or European gun to be marked for chamber length usually on the flats under the barrels. A Belgian gun marked 12–65 means that it is a 12-gauge with 65mm or $2^1/_2$-inch chambers, and one marked 12–70 means that it is for $2^3/_4$-inch cases. If a gun is not marked for chamber length it must be assumed it is for the European standard 65mm cases. The British make few small-bore guns, but instead concentrate on the 12-gauge, making it in many case lengths from 2 to 3 inches and using various shot charges from $^7/_8$ ounce to $1^1/_2$ ounces. On the continent the 16-gauge seems to be the favorite.

CARTRIDGES OF DIFFERENT NAMES INTERCHANGEABLE AND ADAPTED TO THE SAME GUNS

.22 Remington Special
.22 W. R. F.

.25/20 Winchester Repeater
.25/20 Winchester High Velocity   obsolete

.25 Automatic
6.35 Browning Automatic

.32 Automatic
7.65 Browning Automatic

.32 S & W
.32 S & W Long**
                                         obsolete in some brands
.32 S & W Long
.32 Colt Police Positive
.32 Colt New Police

.32 W.C.F.
.32/20 Winchester High Velocity*
.32/20 Colt L.M.R.

.38 Short Colt
.38 Long Colt**

.38 S & W
.38 Colt New Police

.357 Magnum (All .38 Special cartridges can be used in .357 Magnum revolvers, but .357 cartridges cannot be used in any .38 Special revolver.)

.38 Colt Special
.38 Special (.38/44)
.38 Special Target
.38 Colt Special Target
.38 Special Super Police

.38 Remington
.38 W.C.F.
.38/40 Winchester High Velocity*
.38 Colt L.M.R.

.44 Remington
.44 W.C.F.
.44/40 Winchester High Velocity*
.44/40 Colt L.M.R.

.30 Model 1898
.30 Army
.30 Krag
.30 U.S.A.
.30/40 Krag

.30/30 Winchester
.30 W.C.F.

8 x 57 mm. Mauser
7.9 mm. Mauser
7.92 mm. Mauser

.45/70 Government
.45/70 Government Flat
.45/70 Marlin (Lead)
.45/70 Short Range
.45/70 High Velocity

*High Velocity (or High Power) Cartridges must not be used in revolvers or Model 73 Winchester rifles.

**Cartridge so marked cannot be used conversely in chambers designed for the shorter cartridge.

REFERENCE TABLE OF EUROPEAN AUTOMATIC PISTOLS AND AMERICAN CARTRIDGES ADAPTED TO THEM

European Caliber Mark	Corresponding American Cartridge
6.35mm Browning	.25 Automatic
7.65mm Browning	.32 Automatic
9mm (Short) Browning (Corto) (Kurz)	.380 Automatic
9mm Luger (Parabellum)	9mm Luger
7.65mm (Parabellum)	.30 Luger
7.63mm Militaire	.30 Mauser

—From the Western Ammunition Hand Book

3

Changes in the Cartridge Lists

THE LIST OF CARTRIDGES produced by the big American loading companies is in a constant state of flux. New ones are being added almost annually and old cartridges dropped. The reason that cartridges die and are born lies in the good old dollar. Like any other industry in our free economy a company cannot long exist unless it operates at a profit. When sales of any cartridge fall below a certain level, that particular cartridge is being made and handled at a loss. Eventually it will be discontinued. It may be an excellent cartridge ballistically and it may have fervent admirers, but unless it can be sold profitably, it will not be produced.

Why do cartridges lose popularity to the extent that they cannot be profitably loaded? For many reasons. Technological change is one of them. Eighty years ago the vast majority of centerfire rifle cartridges on the lists were loaded with black powder. Today no cartridge or shotshell in America is loaded with black powder, and except for a handful of survivors all car-

tridges designed during the black-powder era from 1865 to 1895 are completely dead.

Some cartridges die through competition with better ones. The .22 Savage High Power, which is now obsolete, was introduced about 1912 and was the ring-tailed wonder of its day, as it drove a 70-grain bullet at the then high velocity of 2,800 fps. It simply could not compete with such specialized varmint cartridges as the .220 Swift, or the .222, etc. The .405 Winchester is another that suffered from competition. When the much better .375 Magnum cartridge was added to the list and the Winchester Model 70 rifle was made to handle it, there was little excuse for anyone wanting a heavy-bullet rifle to buy a .405.

No matter how excellent a cartridge is, sales will not be in sufficient volume to make loading profitable unless rifles are manufactured in considerable numbers for it. The 6 mm Lee-Navy cartridge was a good one for its day and advanced ballistically, but it was doomed when the U.S. Navy dropped it in favor of the Springfield rifle and the .30/06 cartridge and Winchester stopped manufacturing rifles to fire it. The Newton cartridges were and still are excellent, but the last Newton rifles were commercially manufactured in the late 1920s. The .35 Newton vanished from the lists in the mid-1930s, the .256 and the .30 about the time World War II broke out.

The excellent .275 Holland & Holland magnum, a 7mm on a belted case, was dropped from the Western Cartridge Co. lists because it did not sell—and the reason it didn't was that only custom rifles were ever manufactured for it in this country. The sales volume simply wasn't there, and so a fine cartridge died.

All these Remington calibers were introduced since 1950. From left to right they are the 5mm Remington Rimfire Magnum, .44 Remington Magnum, .22 Remington Jet Magnum, .221 Remington Fire Ball, .17 Remington, .222 Remington, .223 Remington, .222 Remington Magnum, .22/250 Remington, .244 Remington, 6mm Remington, .25/06 Remington, 6.5mm Remington, .280 Remington, 7mm Remington Magnum, and the whopping .350 Remington Magnum.

The 7 x 57 or "Spanish" Mauser cartridge has had its ups and downs. It was one of the first smokeless-powder military cartridges. It was adopted by Spain and used by the Spanish in the Spanish-American War. It became known to American big-game hunters through the great quantities of rifles captured from the Spanish. Mexico and several other Latin American countries adopted the 7 x 57, and during the Mexican revolution in the years following 1910 thousands of rifles were brought across the border by defeated soldiers. After World War II when the Latin American countries were rearming with semi-automatic rifles of other calibers, many 7 x 57s in various states of repair were sold in the United States.

Along in the 1920s there was a 7 x 57 boom when Western Cartridge Company and Remington each brought out cartridges loaded with 139-grain bullets at around 2,825 fps in a 22-inch barrel, 2,875 in a 24-inch barrel, and as much as 4,000 in a 30-inch barrel. The standard and very effective load originally was a 175-grain bullet at about 2,350 fps, but in the United States the bullet was stepped up to 2,500. Both were pleasant to shoot. The 139-grain bullet proved very effective for antelope, sheep, and deer.

The pre-World War II 7 x 57 boom resulted in factory rifles in that caliber by Winchester in the Model 70 and Remington in the Model 30. Sales were apparently less than sensational and neither of the big manufacturers makes a 7 x 57 today. The only American-made 7 x 57 is the Ruger Model 77. I have been told its sales are satisfactory.

Today, the 7 x 57 is undergoing another modest boom. One of the reasons may be that riflemen are getting romantic about the caliber used by W. D. M. Bell, the great East African elephant hunter. Another reason is that with proper bullets the cartridge is adequate for all North American big game. It is also fun to shoot because of the light recoil. Federal Cartridge Company and Dominion in Canada furnish cartridges with 140-grain bullets driven at around 2,800 fps in 22-inch barrels. Remington and Winchester-Western load only 175-grain bullets. But the 7 x 57 is still on the lists and very much alive.

In a 1918 Winchester catalog published long after the black-powder cartridges had gone into a decline, I find the .25/20 Single Shot listed, the .25/21, the .25/36 Marlin, the 6mm Lee-Navy, the .32/40 with black powder, the .38/56, the .38/70, .38/72, .40/60, .40/65, .40/82, .43 Mauser, .45/60, .50/110. All of these are now dead.

On the other hand, if a great many rifles are floating around for a certain cartridge it will remain alive for many years after manufacture of the rifles has ceased. Because tens of thousands of old Krag military rifles were sold to civilians for as little as $1.50, the .30/40 Krag cartridge still sells—in spite of the fact that no Krag rifles have been made since about 1900 and the Model 95 Winchester in .30/40 was discontinued forty-odd years ago. Because the ancient Swiss Model 71 Vetterli army rifle for the primitive .41 Swiss rimfire cartridge was exported to this country by the thousands and sold for a few dollars, that miserable cartridge survived for many decades after the manufacture of the rifle ceased. The .45/70 cartridge is still on the lists because so many old Model 1873 and 1878 Springfield rifles are still

Some elderly loads will doubtless go on forever, because so many rifles were once made
for them. From left to right, the .30/40 Krag,
the .44/40, and the .45/70.

30–40 Krag   44–40 Win.   45–70 Gov.

around, and the pipsqueak .44/40 is still made because of the vast number
of old Model 1873 and 1892 Winchester rifles that use it.

An ammunition list published about 1940, before World War II, shows
several black-powder cartridges that are no longer loaded—the .38/56,
.38/72, .40/65, .40/82, and .45/90. All were quietly allowed to die after commercial ammunition manufacture was resumed.

In the decade after World War II, a considerable number of smokeless
powder cartridges were tossed into the boneyard. Among them are the following: .22 Savage High Power, .25 Remington Rimless, .35 and .405
Winchester for the obsolete Model 95 Winchester rifle, the .35 Winchester
Self Loading, and the .401 Winchester. The .405 was dropped once, but
there was considerable consumer protest. The cartridge was then granted a
reprieve, but it sold no better and hence it has been permanently buried.

Other cartridges are in danger. Because no rifles were made for the
.25/35, .303 Savage, .33 Winchester, and .25 and .35 Remington rimless,
they are dead. The .30 Remington lingers on. The .22 Hornet and the .218
Bee compete with the newer and better varmint cartridges, so the Bee is
dead and the Hornet almost dead. The accurate and excellent little
.25/3000 Savage cartridge is not selling as well as it used to. Only rifle made
in the United States for it recently is the Model 99 Savage. The Model 70
Winchester in that caliber has been discontinued, and FN Mausers in
.250/3000 are no longer imported from Belgium. The .348 Winchester
cartridge was not very popular and only one rifle, the Model 71 lever action, was ever made for it. I suspect that the .32 Special is not long for this
world.

Age doesn't have much to do with a cartridge's popularity. Millions of
rifles for the .30/30 Winchester cartridge have been manufactured and in

The .243 Winchester and .244 (6mm) Remington are both fine long-range varmint cartridges and were introduced in 1955.

243 Win.   244 Remington

spite of the fact that the cartridge came out in 1895, it is still a tremendous seller—and so is the Model 94 Winchester rifle chambered for it. Of big-game cartridges for bolt-action rifles, the most popular are the .30/06, the .270 Winchester, which came out in 1926, and the more recent 7mm Remington Magnum. The great .375 H. & H. Magnum cartridge has been in use since about 1912, and the light-kicking but hard-hitting 7 x 57 Mauser cartridge, one that is in use all over the world, came out over 60 years ago and was one of the very first smokeless powder cartridges.

But as old cartridges drop by the wayside, new ones come along to take their place. One of the most sensationally and instantaneously successful ones ever brought out is the .222 Remington, which appeared about 1950. It is flat-shooting, sensationally accurate, easy to reload, gives light report and recoil and is all in all not only a fine 200–225-yard varmint cartridge but a top bench-rest cartridge. It drives a 50-grain bullet at the very satisfactory velocity of 3,200 fps, and traveling to the 200-yard point the bullet has a midrange rise of only 3.2 inches. Remington Model 700 rifles are chambered for the .222 cartridge, and the same applies to the Sako rifles which are manufactured in Finland.

Next biggest news in the way of new cartridge developments was the 6mm twins—the .243 Winchester and the .244 Remington, both of which were introduced in 1955. The .243 Winchester is the .308 W.C.F. case necked to .24, and the .244 Remington is the .257 Roberts case necked to that caliber. Winchester made the Model 70 for the .243 in the light weight, the standard weight, and in the special varmint rifle with a 26-inch stainless-steel barrel. Savage likewise chambers the Model 99 lever action rifle for the .243. Remington makes the standard Model 700 with a 26-inch barrel for the .244. Although Winchester has made rifles for the .243 with 22-, 24-, and 26-inch barrels all velocity figures published are from 26-in. barrels. The same is true of Remington. Winchester rifles in .243 have a twist of rifling of 1 turn in 10 inches. Rifle shooters' fancy did not take to the .244 Remington partly because the 1-in-12 rifling twist would not stabilize a 100-gr. bullet and partly because the original Model 722 was ungainly. It was renamed the 6mm Remington and one twist was changed to 1 in 12, and all was roses.

The .243 Winchester drives an 80-grain bullet at 3,500 fps and a 100-grain bullet at 3,070. The 6mm Remington cartridge pushes a 75-grain bullet at 3,500 fps and a 90-grain at 3,200. Both are excellent long-range varmint cartridges, particularly good on windy days when bullets of .22 caliber are apt to be blown about a bit. For animals the size of deer, antelope, and mountain sheep they certainly have nothing on the good .250/3000 and .257 Roberts cartridges if properly handloaded.

Another Remington success has been the 7mm Remington Magnum. This is simply the .338 Winchester necked down to take 7mm (.284-inch) bullets. Velocity with the 150-grain bullet was at first given as 3,260 fps and with the 175-grain bullet as 3,050. Both were on the optimistic side. The 150-grain bullet in the Remington ballistic tables is listed as traveling at 3,110 fps and the 175-grain bullet at 2,845. The 7mm Magnum has run into the wall called "bore capacity." In other words, you can burn only so much powder behind a hole of a certain size efficiently. Beyond that, pressure goes up faster than velocity and muzzle blast and recoil also go up. I have used the 7mm Magnum on elk in Idaho, on horned and antlered game in

Weatherby's line of magnums is fine if a Weatherby rifle is what you want.

India, and on safaris in Mozambique and Angola. As formerly made, anyway, the 150-grain bullet was a much better killer than the 175'grain. This last did not open quickly enough on medium-size antelope.

The 7mm Magnum is extremely popular and will be around for a long time. I don't believe that holds true for the 8mm Remington Magnum. A rifle for this cartridge has to be made so long and heavy it is laborious to carry. The cartridge gives considerable recoil and would be difficult to shoot accurately. The bullets are not heavy enough for game like buffalo and elephant. As I write this the introduction of the cartridge is very recent but I doubt if riflemen will take it to their bosoms.

The first new Winchester cartridge brought out after the war was the .308. Possibly it would be more accurate to call it the .30 or 7.65 NATO, because it is the cartridge used by all North Atlantic Treaty Organization forces. It was developed by the United States ordnance department and called the T—65.

The .308 is in powder capacity and ballistics about midway between the .300 Savage and the .30/06 cartridges. It drives a 110-grain bullet at 3,340 fps, a 150-grain at 2,860, and a 180-grain at 2,610. The cartridge is, I understand, loaded with Western ball powder. The best things that can be said about the .308 are that it can be adapted to light, fast, and accurate lever-action, pump, and autoloading rifles. It is an excellent cartridge for military use. Otherwise it is in every way inferior to the great .30/06 cartridge.

Winchester based its .284 and .358 Winchester cartridges on the short .308 Winchester case but found that the .284 needed a fatter body to obtain good velocity, and that resulted in a "rebated rim," a rim smaller than the

Remington's Core-Lokt pointed soft-point bullet, left, is designed to mushroom without disintegrating. The Remington Bronze-Point expands when the hard tip drives back into the core; the author has used it in .270 for sheep, caribou, black bear, and moose. The Remington Power-Lokt full-jacketed bullet at right is not designed for expansion and would merely whistle through a deer; it is a target and small-game bullet.

body of the case near the head, something that had been done with English and continental cartridges. At one time I thought something like the .358 would do very well as a cartridge to use on whitetail deer in the woods and that it would catch on quickly. Actually the cartridge had one of the quickest deaths in history. It is not precisely dead today but it is in its death agonies. Winchester chambered the Model 70 for it, and also the Model 88; Savage made the Model 99s, but the boys didn't love it!

The real killer-diller among the newer cartridges is the .458 Winchester, a cartridge based on the .375 Magnum case and one to be used on the world's heaviest and most dangerous game such as elephant, African Cape buffalo, and rhino. Ballistically it duplicates the famous .470 Nitro Express, the favorite British elephant cartridge used in the big and expensive British double-barrel rifles. It gives a 500-grain full-metal-cased, or "solid," bullet a velocity of 2,215 fps with 5,030 foot-pounds of energy and a 510-grain soft-point the same. Since experience of hundreds of hunters on many thousands of big dangerous animals has proved that a 500-grain bullet at 2,000 fps is all that is needed for the toughest creatures that walk, the .458 has achieved a good deal of popularity in Africa.

The cartridge is shorter than the regular .375 and will work through a standard-length magazine. I suspect that a great many rifles in that caliber will be built on standard Mauser, Enfield, Springfield, and Model 70 Winchester actions by custom gunsmiths. As this is written the only factory rifle for the .458 is a Super Grade Model 70 Winchester which weighs about 9 pounds.

The Winchester .264 Magnum has had a rather unhappy history. Designed to be a very flat-shooting plains and mountain cartridge, it was greatly over bore capacity and needed very slow-burning powder and a long barrel to be efficient. It was hard on barrels, and if the barrel was cut to less than 26 inches it gave a fearful muzzle flash. It has never been popular.

4

Rifles for Woods Deer

THE TENDENCY THESE DAYS is toward high-velocity, flat-shooting cartridges with fairly light bullets. Such cartridges are fine for plains and mountain shooting, and I have done my share to promote them. Because they tend to run pressures up, they are generally fired from bolt-action rifles, which often weigh from 9 to 10 pounds after the eager hunter has put a scope on them. Their trajectory is as flat as a stretched string and the good ones will drop all their shots into the crown of a hat at 300 yards.

Many a hunter goes forth with such a rifle to hunt whitetail deer and black bear in the heavily wooded East. From my correspondence I'd guess that thousands of Pennsylvania and Michigan deer hunters carry the .30/06 with the 150-grain bullet or the .270 with 130-grain bullet. Not a few of them have 4-X scopes or even variables on their rifles.

There isn't any doubt that if they make a solid body hit with either bullet the buck will usually go down. If he doesn't die immediately he generally stays down long enough for a finishing shot. Both cartridges are decided killers and most of the bolt-action rifles in which they are shot are very accurate. But does the hunter need all this power, all this accuracy, all this flat trajectory in the woods? I doubt it.

Quite a few riflemen who like a spot of varmint shooting use their .30/06's and .270's in the summer on chucks and in the fall on deer. That's OK, as long as they do it with their eyes open. Others use the .257 or the .250/3000 as a combination deer-and-chuck rifle. Both cartridges produce top accuracy. Both have adequate power for deer. Either is a pretty fair compromise for varmints and game.

But are all these rifles ideal for the woods? Again, I doubt it.

In mountainous Pennsylvania many smart hunters who are also rifle nuts, accuracy fiends, and crack shots find a seat on a point overlooking good deer country. They arm themselves with .30/06s, .270s, 7mm Magnums, or one of the fancier ultra-high-velocity wildcats with 4-X or 6-X scopes.

They have good binoculars to locate deer and to distinguish bucks from does. They scan the open spots and the thin places on hillsides, and when a suitable deer shows up they pour it on. They tell me 300-yard kills are common, and it is by no means unknown for a shrewd rifleman to polish off a buck at 400 yards and over.

Such hunters may do their shooting in the wooded East but they are by no means typical whitetail hunters. Actually they are mountain hunters using mountain rifles. Our run-of-the-mine deerslayer needs no such equipment. He's much better off with a light rifle with fast action and fast sights, one that moves a fairly heavy bullet at moderate velocity and with moderate recoil. He has no need of ultra-high velocity or flat trajectory, for he doesn't knock his bucks off at 300 yards, but usually at less than 100.

Neither does he have any use for the hairsplitting accuracy that enables a rifleman to pick a chuck off a rock at 300 yards, because for the ranges at which most forest game is shot, a rifle that will group into 3 inches—or even 4 inches—at 100 yards is plenty accurate. Most forest game is shot from the offhand position, and the man who can stand on his hind legs and keep his bullets in a 6-inch circle at 100 yards is a very good shot.

Our woods hunter, then, usually shoots at fairly close range, at a large mark, probably moving, and he shoots on his hind legs. That holds true whether he's a still-hunter, a driver, or a stander. Don't let anyone tell you that such shooting is easy. I have missed a higher percentage of bucks with snapshots at short range in heavy cover than I have across open canyons at much greater distances.

Whenever possible, the hunter should rest the gun on a solid object, as in this instance when the author uses his down jacket over a rock for a long shot in fairly heavy brush country.

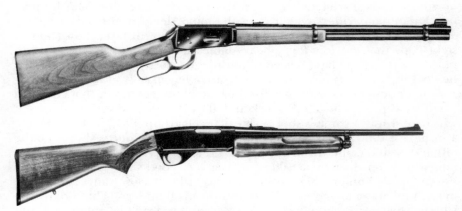

Two fine rifles for deer in brush country, the classic Winchester Model 94 (top) and Savage Model 170-C Carbine. Both chambered for the .30/30 cartridge.

Very often our woods hunter has to shoot through brush, and then no poorer missile can be imagined than a light, sharp-pointed, high-velocity bullet. Some years ago I spent several afternoons shooting at a target—the outline of a deer—through heavy brush with rifles of different calibers and with different weights of bullets. I found that the higher the bullet velocity, the sharper the point, the thinner the jacket, the lighter the weight, the greater the deflection. I also found that the farther the deer was away from the deflecting brush or limbs, the less likely he was to get hit.

My experiments indicated that behind even thin brush a deer is pretty safe if someone is shooting a .220 Swift, and fairly safe even if the hunter is using the 130-grain bullet in the .270 or the 150-grain bullet in the .30/06. But the 150-grain round-nose .270 bullet gave me a much better chance of hitting. Likewise with the 180-grain .30/06 round-nose bullets. The 100-grain .250/3000 bullet was better than the 87-grain, but neither was too good. And in the .257 the 117-grain was superior to the 100-grain.

I concluded, too, that the rotational speed of the bullet may be responsible for a good deal of the deflection, with the bullet spinning away from the surface it touched just as a billiard ball with a lot of English on it spins away from the cushion or another ball.

In reality there is no such thing as a "brush-bucker" among ordinary big-game cartridges. A high-velocity .22 doesn't do too badly but only if the lead core is hard and the jacket tough. Such a bullet will go through more brush than a softer bullet with soft-lead core and thin jacket. The .444 Marlin (or at least those I experimented with) is apparently loaded with revolver bullets with thin jackets and soft lead cores. They often went to pieces before hitting the target. Some foreign shotgun slugs may be all right, but I have never used such slugs as the Brenneke. The American shotgun slug is a hollow shell of soft lead. It was rare if those I tried got through stiff, hard brush.

In Zambia in 1969 my son had almost no trouble with bullets being deflected by brush. He used a .375 Magnum for everything from small antelope through lion to buffalo and elephant. For her "light" rifle my wife used a .30/06, and I a .338. We both had a tough time from deflected bullets. I wound up shooting a lion with a .416 Rigby and a 400-grain round-nose soft-point bullet.

Since the bullet deflects at an angle, the farther the deer is from the obstruction the safer he is. If he is 6 feet behind the brush he is liable to be hit; if he is 20 feet away he is pretty safe.

The old .30/30 cartridge with the 170-grain bullet at 2,200 fps muzzle velocity is good on deer in wooded country. So are the very similar .32 Special, the .30 and .32 Remington rimless cartridges, the old .303 Savage, and the other ".30/30 class" cartridges. None of them can be depended on to knock a deer off his feet with a poorly placed shot, as more powerful cartridges do, but if a man puts a bullet from any of them into the chest cavity or into the neck close to the vertebrae, he has himself a piece of meat. The old .30/40 with the 220-grain bullet is also excellent.

Aces among woods cartridges, though, are the .35 Remington, .300 Savage, and .348 and .358 Winchester. With the 200-grain bullets of the .35 and the .358 and the 180-grain of the .300, the deer hunter gets good penetration, good brush-bucking, and a lot of knockdown power. You need it today in areas where the hunter must get his tag on a buck quickly before someone else claims it, and so these more powerful cartridges are a good idea. The 200-grain flat-point .348 bullet is one of the best brush bullets ever designed and, as far as I could tell from my tests, one of the best brush bullets made today.

Excellent stocked and fast-handling woods rifles in current production are the Winchester Model 70, Marlin Model 36, Remington Model 760, and Savage Model 99s. They have fast actions, handle fast, and are available in good woods calibers.

The man who wants to hunt deer in the woods with a bolt-action rifle can do so, and I'll have to admit that my own all-time favorite brush rifle was a 7-pound Mauser 7mm with a very straight stock and a Lyman 1-A cocking-piece sight. But lever-actions and pumps are preferable because they let you get off a second shot in jig time if your first bullet doesn't get through the brush.

The .270 user should do his woods hunting with the 150-grain soft-point bullet; the .30/06 user with the 180-grain soft-point. Best 7mm bullet for woods use is the standard 175-grain soft-point; best .257 bullet, the 117-grain. I'll undoubtedly be hanged for this, but I think the best and most reliable deer bullets for short range are the old-fashioned soft-points with relatively thin jackets and plenty of penetration on whitetails with any reasonable bullet. With the .270's 130-grain bullet I have shot through three-fourths the length of a deer.

But I've had a good deal of trouble with bullets that opened up *too* slowly.

One lot of .257 controlled-expanding 100-grain bullets I used on a month's hunt in Mexico were really turkeys. They'd go right through deer broadside with practically no expansion, and for that reason I chased wounded deer all over northern Mexico.

With a fancy .30/06 bullet I once shot clear through a big ram from rump to brisket. I didn't do him any good—but I didn't knock him over in his tracks either.

Darnedest thing I ever saw, though, happened with a controlled-expanding .30/30 bullet. An Arizona antelope hunter took a pop at a buck running away. The bullet hit the animal between the hams and went clear through the body cavity, up the neck, and out the forehead between the horns. The buck died, of course, but if our hunter had hit it broadside he wouldn't have known it.

Best iron sight for the woods rifle is a peep; using it, the hunter does not have a tendency to shoot high, as he would do with open sights. The larger the aperture, the faster and better the sight. And the closer the aperture is to the eye (within reason) the faster it is and the more one can see through it. Fastest of all iron sights are the obsolete Lyman and Marble tang and cocking-piece sights. But if you can find one, be sure it is mounted far enough back from the eye so that it won't drive back in recoil and injure the eye. The front sight should be a conspicuous gold bead—$3/32$ or even $1/16$ inch.

Best scope for the woods is one of from 2-X to 3-X. Since it's easy to lose a fine crosshair in poor light against dead leaves and twigs, I'd select a flat-topped post, a coarse crosswire, or a large conspicuous dot subtending 4 or 6 inches at 100 yards.

Because the deer woods are often wet with rain or snow, I like the scope mounted on a deer rifle with a quick-detachable mount. Then, in a pinch, iron sights of some sort can be used. Jaeger mounts are good. So is the novel Pachmayr Lo-Swing. An old and time-tried favorite in this category, and one which I used for many years, is the Griffin & Howe.

While I'm at it, I am going to toss an idea into the air and before you start fighting over it, I'll duck so I won't get hit. This is it: I do not think there is any *ideal* bolt-action brush cartridge for deer and black bears. With the exception of the fine .300 Savage, .348 Winchester, and .358 Winchester, all the standard and wildcat cartridges that have come along in the last 40 years have been ultra-high-velocity super-dupers for plains and mountain use. Deer cartridges have remained about where they were in the early days of smokeless powder. The .30/30 and its running mates could use a bit more velocity and a bit more bore diameter as well as heavier bullets. The .300 Savage and the .30/06 could use more bullet diameter, the .35 Remington more velocity. A 7 x 57 Mauser case expanded to .35 would be ideal, but that would be the old 9 x 57 cartridge.

Our bullet would get through the brush well. It would open up fast, have a lot of shocking power. If it didn't go through an animal it would leave a substantial hole to leak blood and make trailing easy. Recoil wouldn't be bad, and we'd have trajectory flat enough so we could sight in to get a 2-inch rise above line of sight at 100 yards; then the bullet would strike only about 2 inches low at 200. Actually that would make a pretty good moose outfit.

To sum up: Our deer rifle for woods and brush is a specialized weapon—and one that has been kept in the shadow of the ultra-high-velocity hotshots. The man who has a good one, who sights it in properly, and who learns to use it usually brings home the venison.

WINCHESTER-WESTERN'S BIG-GAME RECOMMENDATIONS

Everyone who has ever shot a deer has his own very definite notions as to the effectiveness of various calibers, with various weights of bullets, on different types of big game, and at various distances. Here are the recommendations of Winchester-Western for the use of their various big-game cartridges on game when loaded with soft-point and Silvertip bullets. Since they make the things and since they test them and also hear from many hundreds of hunters annually, they should know a thing or two.

Caliber	Bullet Weight (grains)	Maximum Range (yards)	Recommended for
.250 Sav.	100	200	D
	117	200	D
.270 Win.	130	400	D, A, E
	150	300	E, M
.30/30 Win.	170	200	D
	150	300	D
.300 Sav.	150	300	D, A
	180	300	D, E
.30/40 Krag	180	300	D, E
	220	200	D, E, M
.30/06 Sprfld.	150	400	D, A, E
	180	300	D, E
	180	400	X
	220	300	X
.300 H & H Mag.	180	400	X
	220	300	X
.32 Win. Spec.	170	200	D
	200	300	X
	250	200	X
.35 Rem.	200	200	D, E
.375 H & H Mag.	270	300	X
	300	300	X

Legend:
  D = Deer
  A = Antelope
  E = Elk
  M = Moose
  X = Largest North American Game

5

Bullets for Use
on Deer

LET'S TAKE A LOOK at this most popular and widespread of North American game animals, the deer. Whitetail, mule, and blacktail, he is found all over the United States from the Canadian boundary to the Mexican line. With the exception of a few prairie states, every state in the Union, from Florida to Washington and from California to Maine, hunts some sort of deer. Washington, while we are at it, hunts all three varieties—mule, blacktail, and whitetail. So does Oregon.

As animals go, the deer is not very large. In Arizona the average full-grown whitetail buck will dress out between 85 and 100 pounds. The largest one I ever shot (of the Arizona variety) went $117^1/_2$. In Maine whitetail bucks have been killed that weighed dressed over 300 pounds, but the average Maine whitetail probably does not weigh over 150. The run-of-the-mine Pennsylvania whitetail, because of poor range and overcrowding, isn't too much heavier than his little Arizona cousin.

Largest mule-deer bucks and the largest whitetails run about the same, or something over 300 pounds field-dressed. Blacktails are somewhat lighter. Wherever one hunts deer in North America, though, a buck that weighs 200 pounds field-dressed is a large one, and particularly in the states where any deer with hair on it is legal, the average deer brought in won't weigh 150.

The deer, then, is a relatively small, thin-skinned, soft-fleshed animal. The average whitetail is about the size of an African reedbuck or impala, and the average buck mule deer is about the size of a beisa. Actually many full-grown whitetail bucks are smaller than timber wolves.

The problem in deer shooting, then, is not to look around for a bullet that will give deep penetration but to find one that will open up quickly and reliably. The deer does not have a tough, thick hide to penetrate, heavy bones to break, or great masses of meat to shoot through. In my day I have shot a good many deer, both whitetail and mule deer, at ranges varying from 25 feet to 400 yards or so. For every well-hit deer I have shot and have had to follow up because of insufficient penetration I have been forced to follow several because of too much penetration and not enough expansion.

As I wrote this I can recall instances where well-placed shots failed to put deer down in their tracks—and likewise other game of similar size, like sheep and antelope—but I find it very difficult to remember deer that were not killed quickly because of insufficient penetration. I can remember instances when penetration left much to be desired, but on light frail animals like deer, bullet blowups in my experience seldom affect killing power.

I believe the most sudden-killing deer bullet I ever used was a thin-jacketed, custom-made 120-grain .270 bullet with a core of pure soft lead. I used to load it to about 3,200 fps and almost always when I tagged a deer with that missile he crumpled. I have often had deer hit with it disappear so quickly and completely that I didn't know what happened to them. That was no elk bullet, no moose bullet. I wouldn't try to break a grizzly's shoulders with it, but it really clobbered the small Arizona whitetail deer.

No firmer believer in the world exists than I in bullets that hold together dependably if the game is fairly large. The elk bullet should have enough weight, sectional density, and ruggedness to break an elk's shoulder and to carry destruction well inside the animal. The moose bullet should be one that will shoot through a lot of meat and get inside where the animal lives. Any bullet should have enough power to penetrate so that it won't splatter out on the surface.

However, for relatively light, small-boned, thin-skinned animals like deer, the most effective bullet is one that opens up right now. For shooting at from 200 to 350 yards, a bullet I liked very much was the open-point as made in 130-grain for the .270 by Winchester-Western and in 150-grain for the .30/06.

In the .270, the Winchester-Western Silvertip and the Remington 130-grain Bronze-point bullets have always given me good service. On a trip around the head of the White River in the Yukon in 1945, I used an experimental lot of Remington Bronzepoints in the .270 on Dall sheep, caribou, black bear, and moose with good success.

Of late years there has been a good deal of squawking about the killing power of cartridges like the .30/30, the .32 Special, and even the .35 Remington. When I run it down I usually find that what burns the lads is that they smack a buck right through the chest with a bullet from one of those rifles and the deer takes off. They usually get the deer if they have any skill whatsoever in tracking, but the experience leaves them frustrated and bitter. How come? Almost always, I believe, the answer is that they have been using one of the controlled-expanding bullets which is seen at its best on heavier game like moose, elk, and the largest bear—*not* on little thin-shelled creatures like the average whitetail.

Best bullets for rifles of the .30/30 class are, I am convinced, the old-fashioned soft-point with plenty of lead exposed at the nose and with a thin jacket. The lower the velocity, the greater the amount of lead that should show at the tip, as it is this soft lead that rolls back to mushroom and wreck tissue. With proper bullets the old .44/40 and .38/40 are right fair deer cartridges in the brush in spite of their low velocity and relatively few foot-pounds of energy. Many hunters would not be caught at a dogfight wearing a .30/30, or any rifle of the .30/30 class. I for one consider all of them pretty sad cartridges for people who like to pop away at deer at long ranges. But for ordinary brush and forest shooting at our American deer and at ranges up to at least 150 yards the .30/30 in the hands of a man who can point it is plenty of medicine if a bullet is used that will open up quickly. Most of the time when the .30/30 gets blamed for not enough killing power on deer the fault lies not with the caliber itself but with unsuitable bullets, poorly placed hits, or use at ranges that are too long.

Very often I hear bullets criticized "because they destroy too much meat." I do not know of any bullet that can be considered adequate for deer that will not destroy meat if it is placed where the meat is ordinarily eaten. The man who shoots a deer in the ham with any deer rifle, even a .25/35, will blood-shot a lot of meat. Likewise the man who plugs a buck through the shoulders. On the other hand, he who drives his bullet through the rib cage into the lungs destroys no edible meat whatsoever—even with a super magnum. Plenty of tissue is destroyed, surely, but it is nonedible tissue. The proper deer bullet should, when it strikes the vital lung area, expand rapidly and violently. It should tear lung tissue and cause great shock and hemorrhage.

Plug a deer in the lung area with a quick-opening bullet fired at a good velocity and he seldom travels far. Hit him with a slow-opening bullet that does a minimum of damage and the guy over the hill will probably put his tag on him—or he'll became buzzard and coyote bait.

6

Scopes for the Deer Rifle

AN IDEA HELD BY MANY HUNTERS is that telescopic sights are primarily for long-range shooting, for varmint shooting, and for target shooting. Few realize that the scope is the finest of all sights to use in brush and forest. A correctly chosen scope sight with the proper reticule is also the fastest of all sights on running game. With the right scope and the right reticule accurate shooting can be made in light conditions where aimed shots with any type of iron sights would be utterly impossible.

This enormous advantage the proper scope gives the average deer hunter has never been nearly as widely publicized as it should have been. Once the average deer hunter of the Eastern woods, the Southern brush, and the Pacific Coast rain forest realizes what a superb tool for the job in hand the hunting scope is, scope sales will double. A very high proportion of those who got no deer during their last season wouldn't have been skunked had their rifles been scope equipped.

The scope has a curious quality of apparently seeing through brush. Many times I have become aware that there was a deer on the other side of some brush but I couldn't tell which end was which. All I would be able to see was some hair and a vague form. Almost always a scope would pick out enough detail to show me where the deer's head was, where his vital area lay. Often I have seen deer well enough to shoot them when I couldn't have seen them at all with the naked eye and iron sights.

This ability of the scope to look through brush is something that has to be experienced to be believed. It is as if the hunter could instantly and noiselessly stride half-way or two-thirds of the way to the animal. This quality of the optical sight is important in good light, indispensable in poor. Any scope user has probably made clean, humane kills with his scope under conditions which would have been impossible with any iron sight. This light-gathering power of the scope is particularly important very early in the morning and very late in the evening, those traditional hours when deer are afoot and moving. With a well-selected scope and reticule, the hunter can see to place his shot as a rule about fifteen minutes earlier in the morning and about fifteen minutes later in the evening. Actually under good conditions he can see well enough to shoot by moonlight. I have killed coyotes on the carcasses of dead cattle by moonlight, and in the Far East those who shoot tigers by artificial light from platforms in trees find good scopes infinitely superior to any iron sights.

Back in the days when scopes were far less common than they are now my wife and I went antelope hunting in northern Arizona. On the first morning, when it was still so dark that we had to use headlights to drive, we saw a group of vague white spots on a hillside. With the naked eye it was impossible to tell if they were antelope, domestic sheep, or what; whether they were bucks, does, or fawns. With the $2\frac{1}{2}$-X scope with post reticule on my wife's rifle, she could plainly see that one of the antelope was a record-class buck. She killed it with a single shot. In spite of the fact that there were many hunters and many antelope in the area we did not hear a shot for ten or fifteen minutes, because most of the hunters had iron-sighted rifles and simply could not see well enough to tell bucks from does and to place their shots.

The right scope properly mounted and with the right reticule is the fastest of all sights. With the open iron sight the deer hunter has to try to focus his eyes three places at once—on rear sight, on front sight, and on what he wants to hit. The best open sights with shallow V's or U's aren't bad, but the worst sights, such as the full Rocky Mountain buckhorn, cut out light and distract attention with high and worthless ears which have no more function than the buggy-whip sockets that used to be put on early automobiles. Peep sights are better, but ideally most of them are too far from the eye and the small apertures put way up there on the receiver cut out a good deal of light. Peeps mounted on the tang of a lever rifle or on the cocking piece of a bolt-action are better because they put the aperture much closer to the eye. Precisely how safe they are is open to question at times, but they are faster for brush shooting. But the good scope—ah, that's something else. If using the best aperture sight can be likened to looking through a keyhole, using a

The Weatherby Premier $2\frac{3}{4}$X scope, top, is an excellent fixed-power scope for woods hunting. The Bushnell $2\frac{1}{2}$-8X, if you use a variable-power scope, is fine for deer at its lowest setting.

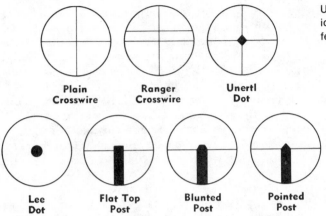

Unertl has a variety of reticule designs for different kinds of shooting.

Plain Crosswire   **Ranger Crosswire**   **Unertl Dot**

Lee Dot   **Flat Top Post**   **Blunted Post**   **Pointed Post**

scope is like looking through a window. The user of the open sight has to try to focus on objects at three different distances at once. The peepsight man has to worry about two—the front sight and the game. But the scope user finds everything (game and reticule) in the same focal plane. His post or his dot or his crosshair is pasted as flat against his deer as if it had grown there. This quality of the glass sight is of enormous importance to the middle-aged and elderly, whose eyes do not have the adaptability of those of the young. The nimble eyes of a kid of eighteen can shift focus so rapidly from rear sight to front sight to game and back again that he is not aware of doing it. The middle-aged man in the bifocal stage finds that if he is focused on the front sight and the game he cannot see the rear. In extreme cases, he cannot see front sight and game clearly at once. Then he either has to quit shooting or get himself a scope.

This business of having everything in the same optical plane and as flat in front of the eyes as a picture or a printed page is of great assistance in quick shooting, and so is the big-window effect of a good scope—or seeing above and below and left and right of the game. Not only have I shot a lot of running big game with scope sights but I have used them to bowl over many hundreds of running jackrabbits and have found them so superior to any iron sights that for that purpose there is no comparison.

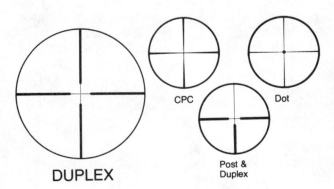

DUPLEX   CPC   Dot   Post & Duplex

Leupold reticules. The Duplex, available from other makers under other names, such as the Bushnell Multi-X, is very popular, combining the accuracy of fine crosswires with the speed-in-use of coarse ones.

Those who think the scope is slow for woods use have used the wrong scope, have had it mounted improperly, or have used the wrong reticule.

Well, what is the right scope and the right reticule? I have heard of good hunters who have used 4-X scopes in the woods and have liked them. I have used them myself—and if the rifle is to be used on varmints as well as big game the 4-X is a good compromise. I would not, however, call the 4-X ideal. Better is a scope of from 2-X to $2^3/_4$-X. All things being equal, the lower the power of the scope the wider the field of view, the greater the light-gathering power, and the greater the latitude of eye relief—all important qualities in the scope to be used at relatively close range, in brush, under poor light conditions, and on animals on the move.

A good modern scope of from 2-X to $2^3/_4$-X will have a field of view of from 40 to 50 feet at 100 yards, as compared, let us say, to around 30 feet for a 4-X and in the neighborhood of 20 feet for the 6-X. In the better American hunting scopes of low power the latitude of eye relief is enormous. The eye will get a usable picture as close as 2 inches and as far away as $5^1/_2$ or 6 inches. This means that the eye does not have to be in exactly the same spot each time and as a consequence aim is quickly caught.

There are many fine scopes on the market with actual power in the 2-X–3-X category—Weaver, Leupold, Redfield, Bushnell, Lyman, etc. All, if equipped with the proper reticule and satisfactorily mounted, are good outfits.

Those making the shift from aperture sights to glass usually like the post reticule because it looks like a front sight seen through a peep. If the post is chosen, it should be of the flat-topped variety with top subtending from 4 to 6 minutes of angle, or from 4 to 6 inches for each 100 yards of range. It can be of the tapered or straight variety and it may or may not be used in connection with a horizontal crosswire.

Another good reticule is the dot, but it needs to be a big one. For all-around use in a $2^1/_2$-X scope for brush and for mountain game I like a 4-minute dot, but for brush use alone in a scope of that power I want a 5- or 6-minute dot. And *that's* something you can see! When a friend of mine was shooting tigers and leopards at night in India by artificial light he used a Lee dot subtending 5 inches at 100 yards in a $2^3/_4$-X Kollmorgen scope and said it was nicely conspicuous.

The fine crosshairs of the target and varmint shooter are absolutely no good for the deer hunter. Neither is the medium-fine crosshair. The medium-fine crosshair in the 4-X that I had on my .300 Weatherby Magnum in Africa was excellent for plains use but in the brush I could not pick it up as fast as I would have liked. On the other hand a *coarse* crosswire is a pretty darned good brush reticule. I had one on a .333 in an Ajack $2^1/_2$-X scope. It showed up beautifully.

Fine crosswires, too-small dots, and pointed picket posts are all to be avoided. So are scopes of high power, small field, and narrow latitude of eye relief.

Many of those who hunt brushy country prefer scopes with detachable mounts giving quick access to iron sights. Others like their scopes attached

A popular scope for deer is the Lyman 2-$\frac{1}{2}$X All American, mounted here on a Ruger Model 77 rifle with Buehler one-piece mount and rings.

with mounts that can be swung quickly aside so open iron sights can be used. Weaver manufactures a quick-detachable side mount and also the "Pivot Mount." The Pachmayr Lo-Swing is a variety of the side mount. One that I have used on several rifles for more than twenty years is the Griffin & Howe. All allow the scope to be taken off quickly so that the top of the receiver is clean. It is then possible to use an open sight on the barrel or to slip in the slide of the receiver sight, the base of which has remained on the rifle—something like the Lyman 48. The Pachmayr Lo-Swing mount or the Weaver Pivot Mount allow the scope to be swung up out of the way so open iron sights can be used.

But I very seriously question the need for auxiliary iron sights under ordinary conditions. In many years of carrying scope-sighted rifles around I have had scopes knocked out only twice by moisture. Once when hunting jackrabbits I got caught in a summer thunderstorm in Arizona and my scope fogged on me. The same thing happened when I had to walk miles in rain through dripping willow and scrub arctic birch at the head of the Prophet River in northern British Columbia.

Nowadays scopes are more nearly waterproof than they used to be. The makers of the nitrogen-filled Leupold scopes claim them to be absolutely fog- and moistureproof and Bausch & Lomb has a similar guarantee. Most good modern scopes are surely very moisture-resistant, and even if a lens should get covered with water a wipe with the thumb will make it usable.

Those who hunt in the West with its open country and its tendency toward long ranges have taken the scope sight to their bosoms. It hasn't caught on so universally in the wooded East. That's because a great many lads simply do not know what they're missing!

The "Widefield" scope in 2-$\frac{3}{4}$X by Redfield is a good choice for deer. The wider field of view with its light-gathering power and greater latitude of eye relief are important in brush, under poor light conditions, and for animals on the move.

The Best Varmint Cartridges

7

READERS ASK why anyone should bother to use a special varmint cartridge when it is no great trick for a reasonably alert person to sneak up on a woodchuck and pot it with a .22 Long Rifle hollow-point. Some have even written me that they have done away with no end of chucks and jackrabbits with shotguns.

The boys forget that the actual assassination of some poor harassed rodent is not entirely the idea. If the killing of the creatures was all that counted, poisoned grain would be more efficient than any rifle ever invented and poison gas pumped under pressure into the burrows would be still more deadly.

Stalking close to a game animal is a lot of fun, but to me shooting some miserable beast at a range so close I cannot miss is no sport. When I have a chance I try to get within certain range on big game, since the stalk along with the trophy head is the reward. But unless the animals are dangerous, the savor is all out of the actual shooting when I am looking down their throats.

The big kick for the real fan of varmint hunting, then, is not the kill, not even the stalk, but the long and difficult shot. With the fast-stepping, quickly expanding bullet, there is almost never a wounded animal, as a solid hit almost anywhere will blow a chuck, a crow, or a jackrabbit to kingdom come. With the varmint hunter, then, it is a clean hit or a clean miss—a pinwheel 5 or a swabbo, as we used to call the shot that missed the whole target and drew the red flag.

This business of reaching out 200, 300 and even 400 yards and blasting down some unsuspecting creature no larger than a domestic cat fascinates a lot of people. Varmint shooting is the fastest-growing of all field sports, and the varmint shooter himself is quite a guy. Manufacturers and custom gunsmiths woo him with fancy new rifles, bright and shiny cartridges, scopes that enable him to see a chuck blink an eye at 250 yards, bullets that all go into the same hole. Everyone now loves our varmint hunter as the soap makers love the housewife.

But this was not always true! When I began shooting varmints in a fairly serious way, anyone interested in the sport was pretty well limited to the choice of two extremes—the .22 Long Rifle hollow-point or a big-game caliber on the order of the .30/06 or .270. The little .22 is a pretty sad excuse for a varmint cartridge and the .30/06 and .270, although they have the range, make too much noise, kick too much, and are difficult to shoot accurately. Back in those dark ages there wasn't any such thing as a factory varmint cartridge. Nearest thing to it was the .25/20. In its standard loading with its 86-grain bullet at about 1,400 fps it was fairly accurate, but it didn't have much more range than a .22 rimfire. In the high-speed form with a 60-grain bullet at 2,200 fps, you could hit your hat at 125 yards—if you had a large hat. Its sister cartridge, the .32/20, was really a turkey and fox cartridge, not a varmint cartridge at all. A few very advanced and sophisticated varmint shooters used the .250/3000 Savage and the now-obsolete .25 Remington, both of which were designed as deer cartridges.

In the past 25 years, though, the factories have devoted as much attention to the varmint hunters as they have to those who hunt big game. They have designed and brought out cartridges loaded with light bullets at high velocity so that standard big-game rifles can be used for varmints—the 110-grain load in the .30/06, the 100-grain in the .270, even a 110-grain varmint load for the .30/30. They have also introduced a rather impressive list of cartridges designed primarily for varmint shooting. The wildcatters have likewise been busy and in the past twenty-five years they have brought out so many off-breed varmint cartridges that 117 private eyes and 26 lightning calculators couldn't keep track of them. I might add that some of them are excellent cartridges.

The .222 Remington appeared a generation ago to fill the gap between the .22 Hornet and the hot .22s like the .220 Swift and the .22/250. Today the Winchester-introduced varmint cartridges like the .218 Zipper and the .218 Bee are about dead. Even the Swift is on its last legs. Remington has been very aggressive in the development of new cartridges since the end of World War II. The .222 has been a smashing success and the .223 has been a successful varmint cartridge as well as the principal infantry cartridge the United States Army used in the Vietnam war. Remington brass also had enough smarts to realize that cartridges which could exist and prosper as wildcats would do even better when produced by factories. They brought out the erstwhile wildcat .22/.250 and .25/06, and these have become very popular. The Winchester-introduced varmint cartridges have not done so well. Like the Zipper and the Bee, the .225 Winchester, which appeared in 1964, is moribund. On the other hand, the .243 Winchester has been more popular than the .244 Remington (now rechristened the 6mm Remington) from the start.

A lot of young American riflemen are going to do their first varmint shooting this spring, so let's take a look at the qualities a good varmint cartridge should have. A great many others are really getting serious about the sport for the first time.

Some high-powered cartridges for varmint. From left to right, the .222 Remington, .222 Remington Magnum, .22/250, .223 Remington, and the 6mm Remington.

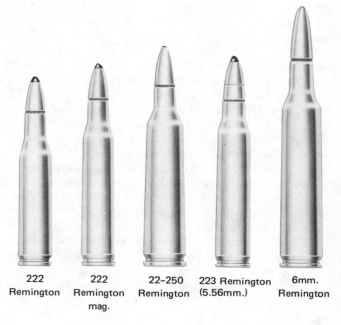

| 222 Remington | 222 Remington mag. | 22-250 Remington | 223 Remington (5.56mm.) | 6mm. Remington |

Of all these qualities, I believe I'd put safety above all. No cartridge is absolutely safe, of course, as the careless, excitable, brainless human being can be as much of a menace with a rifle as he is with an automobile. However, the cartridge that blows its bullet along fast enough so that it goes to pieces when it strikes the ground and does not ricochet off to whine over the heads of indignant farmers and maybe punch a hole in somebody's cow is much safer than the cartridge throwing a slower, heavier bullet that glances. Of all the dangerous cartridges ever made the worst is the mild-sounding .22 rimfire in the hands of a dumb, ignorant, and excitable person. If I had a dollar for every time I have had a glancing .22 bullet whine over my head I could probably take another trip to Africa. Next worst offender to the careless .22 user is the citizen who does his varmint shooting with a .30/06, who does not reload, and who is too fond of a buck to buy factory-loaded cartridges made for varmint shooting. Instead he buys old full-metal-cased and armor-piercing military ammunition. The bullets will glance a mile and sing a merry song when they do so. It is these thoughtless fellows who have loused up the jackrabbit shooting all over the West. It is they who have got the ranchers down on the 99 percent of careful, intelligent varmint hunters. Use of old military ammunition should be confined to the target range, and anyone firing it indiscriminately over hill and dale should be hung by the thumbs.

Probably the next most important quality in the varmint cartridge is a mild report. Most farmers and ranchers are not rifle enthusiasts. They associate noise with danger. If they hear the roaring and booming of a .30/06 in the back forty they are inclined to think that the lives of their wives and young as well as those of their cattle and chickens are menaced by the mys-

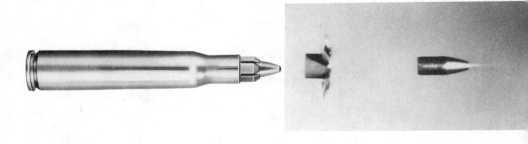

The Remington Accelerator is supposed to make your .30/06 into a small-bore long-range varminter. The .224 bullet is encased in a plastic "sabot," which travels down the barrel with the bullet; a few inches from the muzzle, centrifugal force opens the leaves of the sabot and it drops behind. Muzzle velocity is over 4,000 fps—which is over 1,000 fps more than with the standard 150-grain .30/06 bullet.

terious thing called a "high-power" rifle. They come out with blood in their eyes and chase off the hunter. From then on the place will be posted. The wicked little .22 rimfire is the quietest of all cartridges used on varmints and big bores like the .270 and .30/06 the noisiest. A relatively mild report, then, is almost a must in the varmint cartridge since the varmint hunter does his shooting in land occupied by farmers and ranchers. He hunts close to civilization.

We should look for a safe cartridge that is relatively quiet, and after we have those qualities we can begin to strive for those twin virtues of the varmint cartridge—fine accuracy and flat trajectory. One is no good without the other. The old black-powder .32/40 and .38/55 target cartridges were so accurate that they would lay ten shots into a silver dollar at 200 yards, but they were poor varmint cartridges because of their low velocity and rainbow trajectory. The animals and birds that go under the name of varmints are for the most part small and exceedingly easy to miss. The varmint rifle must put its bullets into a small group and these bullets must fly to the target with minimum deviation from line of aim. Many thousands of varmint hunters have found by sad experience that the less estimating the man behind the rifle has to do the better off he is. The rifleman who has to hold over very far or who has to hold into the wind may guess right, but on the other hand he is more apt to guess wrong.

As far as varmint cartridges go, the very flattest trajectory is none too flat and the finest accuracy is none too good.

Wind-bucking ability is likewise important to the varmint hunter. The longer and heavier the bullet is for its cross section and the sharper the point, the better it will buck the wind. A 180-grain .30 caliber bullet with a sharp point and a boattail such as the match bullets used in .30/06 and .308 rifles for long-range target shooting are very efficient as far as wind is concerned. A short, blunt, light bullet like that of the .22 Hornet is at the other end of the scale.

The .30/06 with a good sharp-pointed 150-grain bullet at a velocity of 2,900–3,000 fps bucks wind well. So does a standard .270 with bullets

HOW THE VARMINT CARTRIDGES STACK UP

CARTRIDGE	Bullet Weight	Velocity	Mid-Range Trajectory 300 yds.	Point-Blank Range	Accuracy	Recoil	Noise	Safety	Suitability for Large Game	Wind-Bucking Ability	Killing Power, Large Varmints	Total Score
.22 LR HP	37 gr.	1365		90	90	100	100	10	0	10	10	320
.218 Bee	46 gr.	2860	11.5	170	90	95	80	80	15	30	25	415
.219 Zipper	56 gr.	3110	8.3	200	80	90	80	80	30	40	35	435
.222 Remington	50 gr.	3200	7	215	100	90	80	90	30	50	35	475
.220 Swift	48 gr.	4110	3.8	260	95	85	70	100	50	50	45	495
.243 W.C.F.	80 gr.	3500		250	95	80	65	90	80	70	95	575
6mm Rem.	75 gr.	3500	4.9	250	95	80	65	90	80	70	95	575
.250/3000	87 gr.	3030	6.4	225	95	80	65	90	80	75	95	580
.257	87 gr.	3200	5.7		95	75	65	90	80	75	95	575
.270	100 gr.	3580	4.5	260	90	70	40	90	90	70	100	550
.270	130 gr.	3140	5.3	225	95	65	40	80	100	95	100	575
.30/06	110 gr.	3420	5.6	230	80	50	40	90	80	30	100	470
.30/06	150 gr.	2970	6.1	225	90	50	40	70	100	90	100	540

TRAJECTORY DATA
.222 Remington—50 Grain Soft-Point

Range in Yds.	Velocity in FPS	Energy in Ft.-Lbs.	Time of Flight in Seconds	Inches Deflection 5 MPH Wind 3 or 9 O'C	Angle of Departure in Minutes	Bullet Drop in Inches
0	3200	1135	0.000	0.0	0	0.0
50	2920	945	0.049	0.2	1	0.5
100	2650	780	0.103	0.8	2	2.0
150	2400	640	0.163	1.9	3	4.7
200	2170	520	0.228	3.6	4	8.9
250	1950	420	0.301	5.9	6	15.0
300	1750	340	0.383	8.9	7.5	23.5
350	1570	275	0.573	13.0	9.5	34.5
400	1400	215	0.574	17.5	12	50.0
450	1260	175	0.688	23.5	15	69.5
500	1150	145	0.811	30.0	18	94.5

TRAJECTORY DATA
.222 Remington—50 Gr. Soft-Point
HEIGHT OF THE TRAJECTORY IN INCHES

Distance from Muzzle in Yards	50	100	150	200	250	300
0	0.0	0.0	0.0	0.0	0.0	0.0
50	0.0	0.5	1.1	1.7	2.5	3.4
100	-1.0	0.0	1.1	2.5	4.0	5.8
150	-3.2	-1.7	0.0	2.0	4.3	7.0
200	-6.9	-4.9	-2.6	0.0	3.1	6.8
250	-12.5	-10.0	-7.2	-3.9	0.0	4.6
300	-20.5	-17.5	-14.0	-10.0	-5.5	0.0
350	-31.0	-27.5	-23.5	-19.0	-13.5	-7.2
400	-46.0	-42.0	-37.5	-32.0	-26.0	-18.5
450	-65.0	-60.5	-55.5	-49.5	-42.5	-34.5
500	-89.5	-84.5	-79.0	-72.5	-64.5	-55.5

weighing from 100 to 130 grains and at velocities of from 3,400 to 3,100 fps. But the recoil is a bit too much for the very finest shooting *all the time*. Ideally the best varmint cartridge should have somewhat less recoil than either. One of the principal reasons for the fine record made by the .222 Remington in bench-rest shooting is the light recoil and the pleasant report of the little cartridge.

The arguments about the inherent accuracy of the various cartridges used on varmints are never-ending, but the accuracy one can get from a 15-pound rifle off a bench rest and with a 25-X scope and the accuracy the same man can get with a 9- or a 10-pound rifle with a scope of from 6-X to 12-X from a prone position in the field are two different things. Practical accuracy is more governed by the condition of the barrel, the bedding of the barrel and action into stock, the choice of bullet, and the amount and kind of powder than it is by case design or even, within limits, by case capacity.

The .222 may be inherently a more accurate cartridge than the .220 Swift or the .22/250. There could be argument between devotees of the two cartridges. There is no argument, though, about the trajectories of the two cartridges. The Swift shoots its bullets flatter because it drives them faster and it drives them faster because it burns more powder.

Even the smaller big-game animals are pretty substantial creatures. A small buck antelope or whitetail deer will measure about 14 inches from the top of the shoulder to the bottom of the brisket. A large deer will measure 18 or 20 inches, a big mountain goat or a large ram 20 to 22 inches, and elk and moose a great deal more.

Because of all this leeway, the big-game rifle can be sighted to put the bullet 3 or even 4 inches high at midrange and no misses will result with a hold behind the shoulder and midway up the body. Used on a large animal, a fairly flat-shooting big-game rifle can be sighted in to have a point-blank range (where the bullet does not rise or fall from the line of sight more than 4 inches) of from a shade over 200 yards in the case of a scope-sighted rifle of the .30/30 class to around 350 yards for a .270 with the 130-grain factory load at 3,140 fps.

With the varmint rifle and the diminutive beasts it is to be used on, the story is something else again and a rifle sighted to put the bullets 3 or 4 inches high at midrange would cause a lot of misses. Many skilled varmint hunters want a bullet rise of no more than 1 inch at midrange, and I doubt if any varmint rifle should be sighted to give more than $1^1/_2$ inches.

Taking a deviation of $1^1/_2$ inches from line of sight with a scope-sighted rifle with the scope $1^1/_2$ inches above the line of bore, the .22 Hornet would have a point-blank range of about 160 yards and the .220 Swift of 100 yards farther or about 260. The other factory varmint cartridges would come somewhere in between.

Whether a rifle is to be used solely for varmints or whether it will have to pinch-hit for big game is another thing that should be considered in a round-up of cartridges. The man who will use a rifle on varmints for only a few days a year and shoots primarily to brighten his eye and steady his trigger finger for the deer and elk season should select his cartridge primarily for its efficiency on big game. For his purposes a .30/06 or .270 would be vastly superior to anything smaller.

Probably the ideal varmint cartridge still isn't with us. I'd like to find one that shot as flat or flatter than the Swift, had the report of the .22 rimfire, the accuracy of a bench-rest .222, the wind-bucking qualities of a 180-grain boattail bullet pushed along at 3,100 in a .300 Magnum. But until such a wonder comes along we're not so badly off.

Ballisticians at the Remington plant at Bridgeport, Conn., have compiled extensive ballistic data on the fine little .222 Remington cartridge for the Model 700 rifle. The cartridge has gained many thousands of fans since it made its debut. It hasn't got the range of the .220 Swift or the popular .22/.250; but it is about 50 yards better than the Hornet and 25 yards better than the Bee. Because it burns much less powder, it is easier on barrels than the Swift or the .22/250, somewhat cheaper to shoot and to reload for, and a better cartridge to use in thickly settled country, since it isn't so noisy.

Because velocities are similar, drop and trajectory figures for the .222 are not so different from those for the .270 W.C.F. and the 130-grain bullet at the shorter ranges. The lighter bullets are, however, more wind-sensitive.

8

How to Select the Varmint Scope

I WAS LIVING IN NORTHERN ARIZONA back in the early 1930s when I got my first varmint rifle—a .22 Hornet. There were many prairie dogs to practice on and I had convinced myself that my life would be ruined unless I got a rifle made to order for them. I did—and then I made the shocking discovery—one that is made every year by thousands of riflemen—that no matter how accurate my rifle was and how flat-shooting *I couldn't shoot it any better than I could see.*

Here I had the latest nine-day wonder, the rifle that had all the gun writers jumping for joy, and yet I couldn't hit prairie dogs much farther than I could with a .22 rimfire. I could pick a dog out from his grass to about 75 yards under fairly poor conditions and to over 100 yards under good conditions. With my aiming equipment, though, I couldn't count on a sure kill on a prairie dog even at 75 yards. The gold bead covered a lot of prairie dog. It shot away from the light. I missed a lot of prairie dogs and I was pretty unhappy.

Then a pal of mine likewise bought a Hornet. He profited from my mistake. Instead of starting out with a receiver sight as I had, he put on the rifle a German Zeiss 2¹/₄-X Zeilklein scope. Now, we both felt, we had her made. But we learned right then and there that there are scopes and scopes. The little 2¹/₄-X was a good big-game scope, but for prairie dogs it wasn't very much better than iron sights. The little glass had a flat-topped post reticule covering 5 inches at 100 yards. With the outfit my pal and I could take dogs consistently at 100 yards, often at 125 yards, once in a blue moon at 150. With it we could hit coyotes to over 200 yards, but we couldn't always kill them.

I decided that the Hornet was underscoped for prairie dogs with a 2¹/₄-X big-game scope, so I invested my hard-won depression nickels in a 5-X target-type scope which is no longer made. It had a crosshair reticule. I experimented around and found that if I sighted my Hornet in with factory ammunition to put the bullet $1\frac{1}{2}$ inches above line of sight at 100 yards, I'd be on the button at 150 and about 4 inches low at 200. I killed a lot of prairie dogs at 150 yards and now and then I'd give just the right amount of Arkansas elevation and plaster one at well over 200. These astonishing feats of the scope-sighted Hornet became the talk of the handful of rifle nuts who pestered the crows, hawks, coyotes, and prairie dogs of the small northern-Arizona town where I was then living. Several other citizens bought scope-sighted Hornets and from then on prairie dogs had a tough time.

I thought I had all the answers for the varmint scope in that 5-X job, but not long afterward opportunity or destiny or whatever it was called me to the southern-Arizona desert. There were no prairie dogs, but there were thousands of blacktail and antelope jackrabbits. Both species are larger than prairie dogs and the shooting they afford is entirely different.

Up on the grassy parks of northern Arizona I had usually shot my sod poodles from prone, sometimes over the hood of a car, occasionally from a rest over a stump or log. Down on the deserts, I hunted jacks by taking off on foot, then shooting those I jumped from the sitting position or even from offhand. I took them on the run about as often as when they were in a stationary position.

BANNER® RIFLESCOPES with Bullet Drop Compensator (BDC) and Multi-X ® (MX) Reticle		MODEL #	Magnification
FIXED POWERS			
		71-3143	10x 40mm
		71-3603	6x 32mm
		71-3103	4x 40mm WIDE ANGLE
		71-3403	4x 32mm

Bushnell's Banner line comes in some useful fixed powers. The 10X at top is a good scope for stationary game. The 6X, 4X wide-angle, and regular 4X are not too powerful for running varmints and can also be used in open country for big game. The variable-power scopes are much more popular, and they do make some sense for the occasional hunter, but the author prefers to use the right power for the job.

Whereas this particular 5-X scope had been all right for stationary targets, it wasn't worth a hoot for the lively jackrabbits. The field was too small and the eye relief too critical. I had a hard time finding a running jack and then when I had found him I often lost him when a slight movement of my head caused the scope to black out before I could shoot.

I found right then and there that there wasn't such a thing as a perfect all-around varmint scope. A glass which is ideal for tracking, passing, and knocking over a coyote or a big conspicuous antelope jackrabbit on the run at 100-150 yards is worthless to the man trying to hold on a chuck on a rockslide at 300. Likewise the scope that will enable the varmint hunter to quarter a crow or a magpie at 250 is no good for nailing a scurrying coyote with a fast shot as he slips through the brush less than 100 yards away.

I get a lot of letters about scopes for varmint rifles, and it is surprising how many people have the right scope on the wrong rifle or the wrong scope on the right rifle. Most varmint hunters learn slowly, expensively, and painfully—just as I did.

A typical example is the lad who starts his varmint shooting with a .22 rimfire. At first he is happy with the 50- and 75-yard hits he gets with high-speed hollow-point ammunition and iron sights. Then he begins to long to make longer hits, to reach out there from 125 to 150 yards to mow down his chucks, his prairie dogs, his ground squirrels. So he buys, let us say, a good 4-X scope and puts it on his .22. He finds he can hit them a little farther but not much. The reason he can't, of course, is that putting a scope on a .22 rimfire doesn't flatten the trajectory one bit. Our boy is still shooting a .22 and putting a high-class scope on a .22 is like putting a $500 saddle on a $15 horse.

On the other hand, a second sportsman reads enthusiastic articles about the .220 Swift and the .22/.250 and how chucks are killed with them at 300–350 yards. So he shoots his roll in the purchase of the dream rifle. Then he decides he'll economize on the scope. He buys an inexpensive little job of about 3-X or 4-X, one that was designed for a .22 rimfire rifle and 75-yard shooting. Then he discovers that the definition of his scope enables him to hit his target only about as far as he could with a .22.

The choice of the varmint scope depends on many factors, then—the sort of varmint mostly hunted, whether it is shot on the sit or on the run, near or far; whether the country is such that the rifleman can shoot prone or from a rest or whether he has to assume a less steady position; what caliber rifle he plans to put the scope on; whether the scope is to be used as a combination varmint and big-game scope or only varmints. Another consideration, naturally, is how much equipment in both rifles and scopes our varmint shooter can afford.

The Redfield "3200" target scope is also a good one for varmints. It is available in 12X, 16X, 20X and 24X.

The Winchester Model 70 Varmint Rifle with a 12X Unertl Ultra Varmint scope.

For the jackrabbit and coyote hunter, a good 4-X scope, exactly the same scope one would use for deer and antelope shooting in open country, is just about right. I have shot hundreds of jacks and dozens of coyotes with rifles equipped with various 4-X hunting type scopes. Within the past few years fine 6-X scopes have come on the market. Hunters in the Southwest particularly have been shifting from 4-X to 6-X scopes for use on running jackrabbits and for big game as well. In some states, a deer has to have antlers to be legal and the lads have found a 6-X on their deer rifles enables them to tell instantly if a deer has antlers or not. They don't have to look with binoculars, then drop the binoculars, pick up the rifle, and shoot.

I have done a lot of rock-chuck shooting with a Leupold 6-X on a bolt-action .25/06 and with a 6-X Pecar on a Model 70 Winchester in .257 Roberts. Both rifles are magnificently accurate and the scopes give me sufficient definition to kill rock chucks consistently to about 225 yards. In the area where I live most chuck shooting is done from automobiles and colonies near roads are pretty sadly depleted. I like to take out my .257, which weighs with scope only about $8^{1}/_{2}$ pounds, and walk from one to three miles back into canyons where the chucks are less sophisticated and more plentiful. The definition of that Pecar is lovely. At 200 yards a chuck is little but he's clear. I have even shot running south Idaho jacks with the same outfit, but for running game a 4-X is better.

Those who dote on making the very longest shots on small stationary targets such as crows and chucks need more power than 6. Hunting-type scopes on rigid mounts are the best if the varmint hunter is going to do a lot of footwork. Fine ones are the Weaver K-8 and K-10, and the Leupold, Redfield, and Lyman scopes of similar power.

These scopes are all of the hunting type. They are internally adjustable for both windage and elevation and are attached to the rifles by rigid mounts. They are strong and it is easy to carry a rifle sighted with them. The real slickers among varmint shooters, the lads who knock over crows to 250 yards and woodchucks to 400, usually want scopes of the target type. These are fixed to the rifle by blocks on the barrel or on the barrel and receiver ring. Windage and elevation adjustments are precise and reliable. Some adjustments are in the mounts and not in the scope tube.

Very often internal adjustments in hunting-type scopes do not respond precisely. Suppose someone with a super-accurate varmint rifle wants to change the center of his group 1 inch at 200 yards. With internal adjustments he may get it and he may not. Instead of being 1 inch, the change may be $^{3}/_{4}$ inch or $1^{1}/_{2}$ inches. With the scope to be used on big game this is

Typical of the new style varmint scopes is the receiver-mounted RM6400 by Redfield, at 24X.

unimportant. With the scope to be used on tiny targets like crows and magpies at 300 yards, this may mean the difference between a hit and a miss. For all their weight and clumsiness, the target-type scopes probably have the most reliable of all adjustments and optically they are surely second to none. They also have the advantage that they can be used on more than one rifle since a record can be made of the setting necessary for each rifle and the micrometer adjustments will bring the sight setting right in.

Ultra-high power is also available in the target-type scope, and many crack varmint shots are not content with the maximum of 10-X available in hunting-type scopes. The fine Lyman Super Target Spot, for example, may be had in 10, 12, 15, 20, 25 and 30-X. My own notion is that 25-X and 30-X scopes are strictly for bench-rest shooting, and that the 20-X scopes are for the small-bore target shots. However, I do know a few varmint shots who swear by the 20-X Target Spot for long-range chuck shooting and many who wouldn't be caught dead with less than 15-X.

For my part, I think that in the target-type scope for long-range shooting at small stationary marks, 12-X is all I'd want. I have a superb Unertl 10-X Ultra Varmint scope on a Winchester Model 70 in .220 Swift caliber. With it I have made more long shots on chucks when conditions are right than with any other rifle I have ever shot. I wish, though, that the scope was 12-X instead of 10. Maybe I'll eventually wind up with a 15-X. The Unertl target-type Ultra Varmint scope is available in no more than 12-X; but Unertl makes a target scope with a $1\frac{1}{4}$-inch objective in powers up to 14, one with a $1\frac{1}{2}$-inch objective in powers 10, 12, 14, 16, 18, and 20-X, and with a 2-inch objective to 24-X.

But such fancy scopes require superlatively accurate rifles, crack shots, and gilt-edged ammunition. The only time I have ever really longed for more power than 10-X was when a couple of compadres and I were trying to knock chucks off across a big canyon at from 400 to 450 yards. We killed enough to keep our hopes up; but I had a sneaking hunch (possibly just an illusion) that I could have made a better average with a scope of higher power. To repeat: *The better you see, the better you shoot.*

A scope simply helps the varmint shot to hold more precisely, to tell what part of the beast he is holding on, and to tell where his target begins and grass, brush, and surrounding territory end. The scope of sufficient definition also enables him to tell a coyote from a dog, a chuck from a rock, and a ground squirrel from a weed. (Once I shot five times at a weed at about 200 yards, thinking it was a ground squirrel. I had a 6-X scope. If I had been using a 10-X I could have told the difference.) But the scope does not make an inaccurate rifle shoot more accurately or a bullet with a curved trajectory shoot flatter. A .22 rimfire with the finest scope ever made on it is still a .22.

It is my feeling that the chap with a .22 rimfire is getting everything out of his rifle that there is in it when he puts a good 4-X scope on it. If he has a rifle of the .22 Hornet—.218 Bee class, a 6-X is all he needs. With a .219 Zipper or .222 Remington, or with a .250/3000 or .257, he is pretty well fixed with a 6-X and very well fixed with an 8-X. With more scope than that he is overscoped, since those cartridges do not shoot flat enough to warrant higher power. In other words, with a good 8-X he can certainly see everything he can consistently hit.

With the flatter-shooting cartridges like the .22/.250, the .220 Swift, the .270 with the 100- and 110-grain bullets, the .25/06 with 87- and 100-grain bullets, the good shot can well go to a 12-X or 15-X scope. But such a scope has its disadvantages. The field is small and the focus is very critical. If the scope is focused for 200 yards, let us say, it is badly out of focus at 100. The small field makes such a scope worthless for moving game. But on a genuinely accurate rifle, a high-power scope of good optics really has what it takes.

The variable-power scope with power from 3-X to 9-X is the best seller in the United States. Many use the variable set at high power for varmints, but this has always seemed to me like taking the girl friend for a ride in a dune buggy.

A suitable scope is just as important for the varmint rifle as the rifle and the ammunition. The most accurate Swift .22/.250, 6mm Remington, or .222 Remington is still just a 100-yard rifle if it has 100-yard sights on it. Putting the right scope on the right rifle is the answer to a lot of the varmint hunter's troubles!

9

All-Around Rifles and Sights

As WE HAVE SEEN, the deer rifle for use in woods should be light and handy and it should have a fast action. The bullet should be of fairly large diameter and easily expanded. Because ranges are short, high velocity and flat trajectory are of no great consequence. The rifle should be equipped with fast iron sights or a low-power wide-angle scope, as an aid in seeing deer through the brush as well as aiming. The cartridge does not need to be particularly powerful, as deer and black bear are for the most part not large animals nor are they particularly tenacious of life.

The all-around rifle is one that is suitable for use on larger and tougher animals at greater ranges—Western mule and whitetail deer, which are often shot at from 250 to 400 yards; antelope, which, although small, are shot at very long range; elk, grizzly bear, mountain sheep, Rocky Mountain goats, moose, and caribou.

It is generally felt that if suitable bullets are used, a retained energy at 100 yards of about 1,000 feet-pounds or about that of the .25/35 is sufficient for a rifle to be used on whitetail deer under ordinary woods conditions. But for all-around use at longer ranges and on larger animals much more power is necessary—1,700 or 1,800 feet-pounds at 100 yards, let us say. At moderate ranges and in the hands of a good shot, the .30/30 is plenty of medicine for most game, but at long range, cartridges of the .30/30 class are not only difficult to hit with but difficult to kill with.

Far better cartridges for all-around use are the .300 Savage, .308 Winchester, .30/06, .270, .300 Magnum, 7 x 57 Mauser, .30/40 Krag, 7mm Remington Magnum or .300 Winchester. In the hands of good riflemen and with the heavier bullets the .250/3000, the .257, and the .243 Winchester and 6mm Remington can be used. For the most part more bullet weight and more power are desirable.

For the very heaviest and toughest of North American game, the .375 Magnum cartridge, with its heavy bullets at fairly high velocity, is made to order. Such game would be polar bear, Alaska brown bear, grizzly, large moose, walrus; but any of these animals, although ponderous, tough, and tenacious of life, can be taken with the .270, .30/06, or .300 Magnum.

For all-around use on any North American big game, from deer in the woods to grizzly above timberline, three cartridges are standouts—the .270, the .30/06, and the 7mm Remington. These are adequately powerful, ammunition is widely distributed, and the recoil is mild enough so that most trained rifle shots can handle them without flinching. Recoil is also such that rifles in that caliber can be built quite light and easy to carry without being so light as to cause excessive recoil. If still less recoil is wanted the little 7 x 57 Mauser cartridge is a very fine one.

Some lever-action rifles are suitable for all-around use—for example, the Model 99 Savage in .300 Savage and .308 Winchester. The Remington Model 760 pump-action rifle in .30/06 and .270 can also be used as an all-around rifle in spite of the fact that the accuracy might be a bit sketchy for the longest shots. For the man who likes the autoloader, the surprisingly accurate Model 742 Remington in .30/06 would be excellent.

But for the most part the all-around rifle is a bolt-action—a Winchester Model 70 or a Remington Model 700. This all-around rifle on a good bolt action is the world's most reliable and simple rifle, the most accurate on big game, and under a greater variety of conditions the most deadly.

For woods hunting, as we have seen, a scope of from 2-X to 3-X is about right, and for varmint hunting on small targets at long range, the prescription is from 6-X to 10-X or even in some cases 15-X. For the all-around big-game rifle, however, a scope of 4-X will be found to be the most useful. The 4-X scope is a fine compromise. It has sufficient definition for a shot at an antelope at 400 to 500 yards and enough field to use in a pinch at 50 yards in the brush. Because of its adaptability the scope of 4-X is the best seller in the United States. With them the latitude of eye relief is usually great enough to enable fast aim to be taken and the field of view of around 30 feet at 100 yards is about right. Good scopes of this class are the Weaver K-4, the Lyman 4-X All American, Leupold 4-X Mountaineer, Kollmorgen 4-X Bear Cub, Unertl 4-X Hawk, Texan 4-X, Bausch & Lomb Balfour 4-X. The Weatherby series of scopes is made in Germany to American specifications. It includes an excellent 4-X. In addition, 4-X scopes in Hensoldt, Ajack, Kahles, Pecar, Bushnell, and Nikel Supra makes are imported from Germany, Japan, and Austria.

Some hunters who confine their big-game hunting to mountains and on open plains prefer scopes of 6-X, but such scopes do not have the versatility of the 4-X. Recently the variable-power scopes have been growing in popularity—the Weaver KV, which can be either $2^3/_4$-X or 5-X, the Weatherby Imperial, which is variable from $2^3/_4$-X to 10-X, the Bausch & Lomb variable that gives choices of power up to 8-X, the Pecar, etc.

The all-around rifle can well have the scope mounted with one of the low, strong bridge-type mounts such as the Leupold, the Redfield JR, the Buehler, Weaver, etc. In a country where there isn't much rain, snow, or wet brush or where the rifle is to be carried on horseback in a scabbard such mounts give maximum support.

If, on the other hand, the hunter wants to have iron sights quickly available, a good side mount or swing mount is in order. An old, time-proved, and most excellent side mount is made by Paul Jaeger of Jenkintown, Pa.

It is similar to the Griffin & Howe, the present status of which I do not know.

Among mounts which enable the scope to be swung out to clear the iron sights are the Pachmayr Lo-Swing mount made by Pachmayr Gun Works of Los Angeles and the Pivot mount made by the W. R. Weaver Co. of El Paso.

How much the all-around rifle should weigh depends on the type of country the rifle is to be carried in and the physical condition of the man who carries it. I have seen the time when I could carry 10$^1/_2$-pound rifle through the roughest montains of North America day after day and not mind it. I am not as young as I used to be and a rifle that weighs 8 pounds complete with scope and sling now seems much better. Actually a rifle need not be heavy to shoot well. My favorite mountain rifle today is a Model 70 Winchester in .270 Caliber that has been remodeled and res-tocked in fine French walnut by Al Biesen, the Spokane, Wash., stockmaker and rifle builder. Barrel is 22 inches in length. Scope is a Kollmorgen 4-X Bear Cub on Tilden mount. The little rifle will shoot a 1-inch group from a rest with almost any good bullet and it will put all full-power loads into pretty much the same point of impact at 200 yards. The big-game hunter has no use for greater precision.

A .30/06 can be made as light and a 7mm a bit lighter. For all-around use I would not want a rifle to be much lighter and I wouldn't want a barrel shorter than 22 inches. Shorter barrels result in muzzle-light rifles that are hard to hold steady and in increased and unpleasant muzzle blast. My Winchester Model 70 in .300 Magnum with Kollmorgen 2$^3/_4$-X scope on Griffin & Howe mount weighs 10 pounds and I would not want it lighter.

By all means the all-around rifle should be equipped with a shooting gun sling like the widely used $^7/_8$-inch sling of the Whelen type, an easily adjustable one-piece job. I much prefer quick-detachable swivels of the Winchester type. The same swivels but on a smaller scale are made by Paul Jaeger, the Pennsylvania gunsmith, and by Uncle Mikes of Portland, Oregon.

This all-around rifle, then, can do a lot of jobs. It is just about the answer for most running shooting of coyotes or jackrabbits. It has the range and accuracy for a buck antelope at 500 yards, power enough for grizzly bear and moose, and it is light enough to carry around in the mountains for sheep and goat.

I have a .270 which is now over forty years old. I don't use it much any more as it weighs 9$^1/_2$ pounds with scope and sling and that's getting a bit heavy for me to lug in rough country. But with that one rifle I have done a lot of hunting. It has a Lyman 2$^1/_2$-X Alaskan scope on the now-obsolete but still excellent Noske side mount. It is now on its third barrel and I have probably fired it at least 10,000 times. I have carried it from Sonora to Alaska, and with it I have shot 10-pound jackrabbits and 1,600-pound moose. I have killed all four varieties of North American wild sheep with it, grizzly and black bear, caribou, mule and whitetail deer, goat, coyotes, wolves, javelinas, elk, antelope, and everything that walks this continent except brown bear and musk ox. It is *really* an all-around rifle!

10

The Controversial .270

THE .270 WINCHESTER CARTRIDGE has been around for a little over fifty years. In that time it has become and remains one of the most successful and popular of American cartridges designed for big game. Other cartridges of the same age or even younger are now pretty well forgotten but the .270 goes rolling along.

The .300 Savage, which was once very popular, is now well down on the lists. The .300 H&H Magnum, which appeared in a factory rifle much later than the .270, is now just about dead. The good .257 Roberts had a reign of about twenty years (from 1934 to 1954) but is about finished. A whole covey of hotshot .22s has perished—the .22 Hornet, the .218 Bee, the .219 Zipper. Even the fine .220 Swift is barely breathing. The .358 Winchester never made it and the 6.5mm and .350 Remington Magnums have flopped. The good .284 Winchester and .280 Remington are only feebly alive. What will be the fate of the 8mm Remington Magnum I cannot say but if I were betting I'd give odds that it will not be around in ten years. The .264 Winchester has not done well, but the .338 has found limited acceptance.

The .270 is available in about all makes of rifles foreign as well as American. It appeared first in 1925 in the Winchester Model 54, the predecessor of the famous Model 70. The Sedgley Springfield, a semi-custom mass-produced rifle made in Philadelphia, was chambered for .270 as well as for the .30/06 and other calibers. The second American factory rifle for the .270 was, I believe, the Remington Model 720, a revision of the Model 30. It appeared about the time World War II broke out. Since that time Remington has made .270s in the bolt-action Models 721, 725, and 700 and the slide-action Model 760; Savage in the Model 110; and Ruger in the bolt-action Model 77 and single-shot Number One. Browning has delivered .270s in bolt-actions, single-shots, and the semi-automatic BAR. Rifles in .270 have also been turned out by High Standard, Colt, and Weatherby.

The .270 Winchester next to the somewhat larger 7mm Remington Magnum. Both are fine cartridges and both have their fans, but the author leans toward the .270, which has the same practical effect as the 7mm but kicks less. The 30-06 on the right is about all you'd ever need for North American big game—except possibly Alaskan brown bear. It has Remington's 180-grain pointed soft-point Core-Lokt bullet.

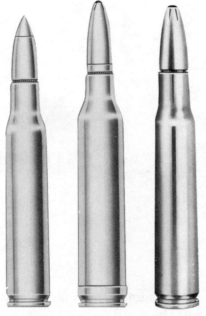

270 Win.   7mm. Remington   30-06 Sprg.
mag.

In Europe .270s have been made by Husqvarna of Sweden, Schultz & Larson of Denmark, Sauer of Germany, FN of Belgium, Birmingham Small Arms and Parker Hale of England, CZ in Czechoslovakia, and Sako of Finland.

A few .270 double rifles have been made by Westley Richards of England and by Belgian, Austrian, and German custom gunsmiths. In 1969 when my wife, our son Bradford, and I were returning from a thirty-day safari in Zambia we encountered an attractive Spanish couple on our plane who were on their way to Rome after a safari in another part of Zambia. The man had shot a lion, a leopard, and all his antelope with a Westley Richards .270 double. In 1967 when my wife, our son, and I flew into a lake in the Cassiar district of northern British Columbia we encountered an Italian and an Austrian, who were also hunting Stone sheep. The Italian had a side-by side .270 double, the Austrian a .270 over-and-under. As a grouse gun and a spare rifle the two shared a combination gun—a .270 barrel over a 20-gauge.

Many custom rifle makers say they build more .270s than any other caliber. Al Biesen, the Spokane, Wash., genius, told me recently he made more .270s than all other calibers put together. Jerry Fisher of Kalispell, Mont., and Len Brownell of Sheridan, Wyo., both crack rifle makers, have in the past said about the same thing. Right after World War II the troubled but prestigious firm of Griffin & Howe, New York, was building more .270s than anything else, but the last I heard the favorite was the 7mm Remington Magnum.

The first ten years it was on the market the .270 set no records. It began to catch on around the middle 1930s. Colonel Townsend Whelen, dean of American gun writers, was a user and a booster of the .270. So was Monroe H. Goode, the gun editor of *Sports Afield,* and Russell Annabel, famous outdoor writer who was long an Alaskan sourdough but who now lives in Mexico.

I got my first .270, a Model 54 Winchester, in 1925. I was intrigued by its high velocity with the 130-grain bullet at 3,160 fps, its flat trajectory, and its fairly light recoil. I shot some mule deer and a couple of antelope with this rifle, but I never had a scope for it and did not fully realize its potential.

It was my second .270 that converted me. It had a Sukalle barrel and commercial flat-bolt Mauser action, a stock by Alvin Linden, the fabled Wisconsin Swede stockmaker, and a $2^1/_2$-X Noske scope and Noske side mount on a Pachmayr base. I sighted this rifle in to put the 130-grain bullet 3 inches high at 100 yards, 4 inches high at 200, on the button at about 275, and about 2 inches low at 300. The scope had a 4-minute Lee dot reticule. All I had to do was to slap that dot on what I wanted to hit and squeeze the trigger.

When the .270 came out it was regarded as a "deer, sheep, and antelope" cartridge because of the 190-grain bullet. For elk and larger game it was supposed to be strictly a no-no! After all, it is logical to assume that for big animals you need big bullets, just as it is also logical to assume that strong liquor makes strong men. When the .270 first appeared and before he had used it on game, Colonel Townsend Whelen wrote that it would probably be better with a 150-grain bullet.

In the 1930s and early 1940s I was shooting a lot of deer, mostly Sonora whitetails, with the .270. I used Winchester factory loads with the 130-grain bullets and also Barnes 120-grain soft-points at a velocity of about 3,200 fps in Western cases with 52 grains of No. 4064. Mule and whitetail deer, antelope, and sheep were killed instantly in their tracks with lung shots. Like many others I considered the 130-grain bullet too "light" for the larger animals.

I began changing my mind in 1943 when I went on my first hunt in the Canadian Rockies. I have told this story before but I'll tell it again. I had never shot a moose and I was in a swivet to get one. When I did not get a shot after four days of hunting moose with a .30/06 I decided to change my luck and use a .270. Hunting alone in heavy forest, I stumbled onto a big bull lying down. My first shot knocked down a shower of twigs and small branches, but my second was in the open and I called a shot behind the last rib on the left side with the bullet to angle up toward the right shoulder. The bull ran maybe 40 yards and went down in a patch of arctic willow. As I approached he lurched to his feet and I shot him again. It seemed to me that the .270 would do for moose.

Since that September day in 1943 I have shot with the .270 caribou, goat, black bear, grizzly, elk, pronghorns, eleven other moose, all varieties of North American sheep, javelinas, coyotes, and whatnot. I have made several dozen pack trips from the Arizona Sierra Anchas to the Yukon's Pelly mountains. On these I have used almost entirely the .270 and the .30/06. I have also used the .270 in India on various deer, black buck, and wild boar, in Iran on wild sheep, ibex, and boar, and on safaris in Botswana, Chad, and Kenya. I have also used on eleven African safaris the .30/06, 7mm Remington Magnum, 7 x 57, .257 Weatherby, .300 Weatherby, .338 Winchester, .375 Magnum, the wildcat .458 Watts, .416 Rigby, .450/400 Jeffery double, and .222 Remington. Don't let anyone tell you that pound for pound African game is harder to kill than North American game. It isn't. A .270 bullet in the ribs will put down the eland, an antelope often as large as a Cape buffalo. The greater kudu is about the size of a spike bull elk, the gemsbok and the white oryx somewhat smaller. I have taken or seen taken all of these animals with one shot with the .270, the 7 x 57, the .30/06, and the 7mm Remington Magnum. With either the 130-grain or the 150-grain bullets the .270 is a fine all-around big-game cartridge. I have never shot a lion with a .270 but I have never had a .270 at hand when I encountered a lion. My friend Bob Lee, a New Yorker of vast African hunting experience, has shot nine lions with the .270 and the 150-grain Nosler bullet.

Today the .270 after a half-century is still one of the most popular of big-game cartridges. I believe the .30/06 is still the best seller among rifles chambered for big-game cartridges. The .270 belongs in the company of such great "world" cartridges as the .30/06, the 7 x 57, and the .375 even though the .30/06 probably outsells it and the 7mm Remington Magnum also probably does. The .243, which is used on varmints as well as big game, is also very popular.

The 7mm Remington Magnum is a fine cartridge. I have shot more game with it than many who swoon in their beer at the mention of the name. I used it as a "light" rifle on safaris in Mozambique and Angola in 1962, in India in 1965, and in Idaho on elk. I found it particularly deadly with the 150-grain Remington Core-Lokt pointed soft-point bullet. Theoretically it should have a little more killing power than the .270. It uses heavier bullets at somewhat higher velocity, but if there is any *practical* difference I have not seen it.

The .270 has certain advantages over the 7mm Magnum. It kicks less. The magazine holds one more cartridge. The .270 can be lighter and still not have objectionable recoil. A very accurate .270 can weigh with scope 8 pounds or a little less and have a 22-inch barrel. A 7mm Magnum should weigh 8½ or 9 pounds and have a 24-inch barrel. Shoot a 7mm cartridge in a 22-inch barrel and any difference in velocity between it and the .270 is peanuts.

In spite of a half-century of successful use all over the world, the .270 is still to some extent a controversial cartridge. Ever since the cartridge appeared it has outraged the believers in heavy bullets and big bores. Since I was an early user of the .270 I read with interest almost fifty years ago in *The American Rifleman* an article by a Montana man who said the .270 was a "joke on elk." Since I had at the time never shot anything larger than a deer with the .270 I wondered if the guy might be right. Just why the .270 was a joke I did not know—and the writer did not say. He did not bother to tell where the animals that presumably got away were hit, how far they went, or anything else.

This sniping at the .270 has gone on in a similar vein ever since. Generally the criticisms are in the form of flat statements. Many times they are by people who have never had any experience with the .270, and sometimes they are by people who have had little experience with anything.

In an article in a gun magazine a .270 hater said he tried the .270 when it first came out and found it a real disaster. It "failed miserably on elk," he said. In fact he found the original Winchester 130-grain bullet such a flop that he "refused to guide anyone for elk who carried a .270."

Now I have been using the .270 on various game animals and in various places for a long time. My experience has differed so radically from this good man's that it makes me wonder if we are talking about the same cartridge. Not everyone has found the .270 a flop on elk. Twenty-five years or so ago the late Lucien Carey, one of the most gifted writers ever to write pieces on guns, published in *True* an article on a member of the Colorado Game Department who shot hundreds of marauding elk on "control." His favorite elk cartridge? The .270! His favorite elk bullet? The old 130-grain Western open-point. This combination was also the choice of John George, a Lewiston, Idaho, elk guide and hunting-camp owner. Likewise of Jack Wirtz, a Clyde Park, Mont., guide and outfitter.

But back to the denunciation of the .270 as an elk cartridge by that sturdy old Western guide. I would like some particulars before I swallow the statement. Just what went wrong? Just how did the .270 fail so miserably on elk? Did the bullets bounce off like hail off a tin roof? Did they simply disintegrate into puffs of white smoke when they struck elk hair? Or did they explode in fiery balls of different colors like Roman candles? I would like some particulars.

Saying the .270 (or any other cartridge) is "a miserable failure" requires explanation and amplification. It is like the blanket statement that Sally Jones is "not a very nice girl." Just why ain't ole Sally nice? Does she run away with other women's husbands? Does she partake too freely of the grape, grow rowdy, shout ribaldries, and in general make a damned nuisance of herself? Does she dance nude in the rain on summer afternoons? Let's get with it! Let's lay it on the line! Just *why* is little Sally Jones naughty and *why* did the .270 fail on those iron-plated elk?

Some of the denunciations of the .270 are so ridiculous that it is difficult for me to believe that those who make them have had anything but the most superficial hunting experience. One character writing in a now-defunct magazine told of the black bear shot through the lungs with a 130-grain .270 bullet that climbed a tree, took four more .270 bullets in the lungs, then a .300 Magnum bullet in the lungs and another in the neck before it fell out of a tree. Another lad wrote of an elk shot smack in the middle of the neck with a .270 bullet as it faced the hunter at 100 yards. The elk ran a half-mile but collapsed when it was climbing a hill. It was still alive when found. The elk was not knocked down! In my day I have probably seen one hundred animals shot in the neck. All fell! Those not hit in or near the neck vertebrae often got up and wobbled off, but all fell.

Another character who considers the .50-caliber machine-gun cartridge about right for elk says he has seen elk full of .270 bullets galloping around not greatly bothered. Another writer says he was at a camp where a hunter used a .270 to knock down a bull elk with a lung shot. The bull got up and ran off. It was killed by another hunter a few days later and recognized by a "peculiar antler formation." I would be willing to bet $10 against a stale ginger snap that this tale is pure baloney. It is very, very rare that an animal ever falls to a lung shot and then gets up.

Most game gets away from poor shooting by unskillful and excited hunters. They shoot from unsteady positions and at too great a range. They yank the trigger. They bang away at the animal's hind end. They are too inexperienced to recognize a hit and too lazy to go and make sure they have missed.

Poorly selected bullets can also lead to failure. Back in the 1930s some .30/06 owners tried to save a few cents on deer hunts by doctoring full-metal-jacketed military bullets so they would expand. The makeshift bullets often did not work. They wounded because they went through without expansion. A varmint bullet with a thin jacket and a soft lead core is generally not much good on big game. Expansion is premature and excessive. Wounds are often shallow. Full-metal-jacketed bullets such as those made for thick-skinned game do a poor job on soft-skinned game because the bullets do not open up, tear tissue, and cause bleeding. I was once forced to do some shooting of African antelope for camp meat with .375 "solids." Unless I managed to hit bone the bullets had little immediate effect.

A bullet too heavily constructed for the game is likewise unsatisfactory. Elsewhere I have written of a ram hit from above and behind the shoulder by a bullet that penetrated a lung and came out the brisket with no expansion. The ram needed another shot. The bullet was made especially strong for use on elk.

Many a heart-breaking tale comes about because the lads miss or wound an animal through poor shooting. They then come back with tales of bucks or bulls that were well hit but ran off with blood spurting and were never seen again.

Or they make them up to prove a point. Time after time I have read or heard stories of animals getting away that were sorely wounded with well-placed shots from light rifles. The narrator then shakes his head and says it comes from using too light a rifle, that if a bullet of .32 caliber or larger had been used the animal would have perished on the spot.

Stuff and nonsense! When I check up on the tales I find that the stories have been made up out of thin air or the shot was poorly placed. The notion that if you use a big heavy bullet you can hit the animal almost anywhere and get him is pure moonshine.

A friend of mine who has outfitted for big game for many years tells me that hunters who go back into the mountains with .270s are generally good hunters and good, careful shots and conservative by nature. This particular outfitter says he jumps like a spooky horse when one of his dudes arrives with a super magnum hell-blaster. Such guys, he says, may be good hunters and good shots, but the chances are that they try to depend on foot-pounds instead of shot placement. He also says that he has seen more game wounded with the big blasters than with any other class of cartridges. He says those who own them are afraid of them and do not practice.

The big-bore/small-bore controversy of which the .270 is a part has been going on for a long time. It is very one-sided. It is the big-bore boys who are always backing the users of small bores into corners and telling them they are inadequately armed and leave the woods full of wounded animals. Most .270 and .30/06 users don't give a damn what anyone else uses. If Oscar K. Jukes, the famous Pike County bear hunter, wants to shoot elk and moose with a .600 Nitro Express it is OK by them. They figure just about any bullet in the right place will do the trick.

But the big-bore boys are always on the prod. They are after the small-bore users like a ferret after a rabbit. One guy has been bugging me for years, bombarding me with reams of phony quotes and ballistics.

Most of my big-game hunting is behind me, but what I'll do in the future I'll do with a .270 Model 70 Feather weight Winchester with a 22-inch barrel. It began life as a run-of-the-factory Featherweight. I sent it to Al Biesen. He put a release button in the trigger guard for the hinged floorplate, restocked with a piece of French walnut I had gotten from P. O. Ackley, and fitted a Leupold 4X scope on the now-obsolete Tilden top mount. The rifle has only changed point of impact once since I have had it. About two years ago it started shooting an inch high and I brought it down. With 62 grains of Bruce Hodgdon's war-surplus No. 4831 behind the 130-grain Nosler bullet it will deliver about 3,140 fps and stay within an inch. With it I have shot whitetail deer, three rams, elk, caribou, grizzly, mule deer. I carried it on a safari in Botswana and shot elk-size kudu, giant oryx, zebra, and smaller stuff.

If my creaky joints and clouded eyes are up to it I'll take it whitetail and antelope hunting next fall.

11

Just How Good Is The .30/06?

MANY OTHER CITIZENS have shot more game with the .30/06 than I have, but I believe I've done enough hunting with rifles chambered for that cartridge to have more than a fair idea about its capabilities. I started shooting a .30/06 back in 1914 when I was a bright-eyed lad of twelve, and I've been using .30/06 rifles ever since. I have shot the little Southwestern wild pigs, called javelinas, with the .30/06—and they weigh about 40 to 50 pounds on the hoof. I have also shot Alaska moose with it, and they weigh 1,500 pounds or more. With the .30/06 I have killed eight grizzlies, two elk, assorted mule and whitetail deer, black bears, antelope, caribou, and mountain sheep, as well as African game.

A big bull mountain caribou doesn't miss being as large as a bull elk by very much, and I once polished off two such bulls with three shots—all hits—at right around 400 yards with the humble .30/06 and the 180-grain Remington pointed soft-point Core-Lokt bullet. My first shot, from the prone position, hit one bull right through the lungs. He ran about 10 yards and fell. I swung over to the second bull, fired, and heard the bullet strike, He ran about 30 yards and stopped. I shot again and he went down with both shoulders broken. The second shot was, I believe, unnecessary. Those two bulls lay dead not 50 yards apart. Why? As in *any* big-game shooting, placement of shots is vastly more important than the bullet used. Those caribou went down because they were hit right, whereas if they'd been shot in the paunch with a .375 Magnum they would probably have given me a long chase.

One of the hot-stove-league arguments now going on is whether the .30/06 or the .270 is the better big-game cartridge. I have hunted for years with both calibers. Right now I have three .30/06s and three .270s. And that, I believe, shows how I feel.

As I see it, the 200 fps greater velocity of the 130-grain .270 factory load gives it a *slight* edge over the 150-grain .30/06 on lighter animals like deer, antelope, and sheep. This .270 load also has a somewhat longer point-blank range, 275 yards or thereabouts when the rifle is sighted in to put the bullet 4 inches high at 200. The point-blank range would be 250 yards in the .30/06. A somewhat higher impact velocity at the longer ranges gives the .270, I believe, a higher percentage of instant kills than the .30/06. Flatter trajectory plus slightly less punishing recoil means that many hunters can do more accurate shooting with the .270.

On the other hand, the .30/06's heavier bullets make it a little superior on the larger animals. So while it's my belief that the .270 has the edge on lighter game, I'd give the .30/06 the nod on heavier animals. I doubt that anything that can be put through a .270 would be quite as effective on the heavier stuff as a good 180-grain bullet in the .30/06. And when a man is hunting really heavy and potentially dangerous game I don't think any .270 load is as effective as a good 220-grain bullet in the .30/06, as these babies play for keeps and the bullet must drive into the vitals at all costs.

I used to believe—with many another—that the .270 is inherently a more accurate cartridge than the .30/06. And indeed at one time there were more .270 rifles of gilt-edge accuracy than .30/06s of the same class. Now I'm inclined to believe that such accuracy (in either caliber) was due to certain excellent bullets and to individual outstanding rifles. Before the war the only .270s floating around were high-class Model 54 and Model 70 Winchesters, plus some top custom rifles. Contrariwise, there were all sorts and conditions of .30/06s in existence. But today you run across .270s that are good, bad, or indifferent. A good .30/06 is good, and a bum .30/06 is lousy. But the same thing applies to the .270!

Put it this way: any good rifleman can take any North American big-game animal with either the .270 or the .30/06 if he has suitable bullets. If I were hunting antelope in Wyoming I'd prefer the .270, and if I were hunting big Alaska brown bears I'd prefer the .30/06. But if I had to shoot a brownie with a .270, I'd load up with the 160-grain Barnes bullet and 52 grains of No. 4350, or simply take the Remington 150-grain soft-point Core-Lokt factory load and go to it. With that last load, incidentally, I wouldn't feel helpless taking a long shot at a Wyoming antelope.

Part of the criticism of the .30/06 is rooted in the use of unsuitable bullets. For many years I lived in the Southwest, where the most popular game animal is a little whitetail deer whose weight averages about 100 pounds field-dressed. Also on the menu were antelope, which weigh about the same, javelinas that dress out at from 25 to 40 pounds, and mule deer that dress out at an average of 200 pounds. Most of the smart riflemen who, twenty years ago, used the .30/06 wanted the 150-grain bullets. Were they easy to get? Brother! The store shelves were loaded with 180 and 220-grain factory cartridges, but the fast-stepping, quick-opening 150-grain was hard to come by—practically under-the-counter stuff. When the word got around that a certain store had stocked some ammunition loaded with 150-grain bullets, the .30/06 fans would rush there and buy a few boxes while the buying was good.

The 150-grain factory loads at a muzzle velocity approaching 3,000 fps are incomparably the best medicine in the .30/06 for longish ranges on light game like deer, antelope, and sheep. The man behind a scope-sighted

.30/06 can carefully sight in to put his group 3 inches high at 100 yards. He'll then be 4 inches high at 200, on the nose at about 250, and 5 inches low at 300. Up to 250 yards or so, one of those 150-grain bullets in the chest of a deer-class animal almost always means an instant kill. I have used the old Winchester pointed-expanding bullet in that weight, the U.S. copper tube, the Remington Bronze Point, and the Western open-point. All were good. Of the bunch, the U.S. bullet was the slowest to open, the Western open-point the fastest. Once I shot a coyote with that Western job at no more than 50 yards, and the bullet didn't even get through to the far side. The inside of the coyote was a mush. I saw a friend smack a running white-tail buck in the neck, and that fast-opening bullet almost took the whole neck off.

For animals of this class the 150-grain bullets are the quickest killers in the .30/06, and offer the best chance to anchor game with poorly placed shots. Out at and beyond 200 yards, they'll usually knock a deer down, while the heavier, slower 180-grain bullet often puts a deer down only to let him get up and run anywhere from 25 to 200 yards.

If 150-grain ammunition for the .30/06 had been well distributed in the Southwest, I doubt that the .270 would have had its tremendous popularity there. But when lads using the 180-grain .30/06 stuff saw someone with a .270 reach out and bounce a big buck at 300 yards they'd naturally be impressed. The .270 owes its rise to fame and fortune in the mountain states to the fact that in spite of hell and high water you simply could not, for many years, get any other ammunition than that loaded with excellent 130-grain bullets. If its original load had been the 150-grain bullet at 2,800 fps it would have become about as popular as the 7mm.

The 180-grain bullet is the best for *all-around* use in the .30/06. It does pretty well on whitetails and such, but don't let anyone tell you that it gives as high a percentage of instantaneous kills as the 150-grain .30/06 bullet or the 130-grain .270. Most 180-grain bullets are constructed to hold together. That kind of construction, plus the moderate impact velocity of the 180-grain bullets, simply does not permit the blasting effect produced by the fragmentation of lighter, faster bullets. The 180-grain bullet does better on larger animals, like elk and big bull caribou, simply because they have more bulk to slow up the bullet and permit it to expand into a flesh-shattering slug.

I mentioned the quick kills on those two bull caribou. On the same trip I shot a big Dall ram in the upper part of the lungs, and he stayed on his feet, giving no sign of having been hit, for five or six seconds before he toppled over. I shot a desert sheep through the lungs with a 180-grain .30/06 bullet and he too seemed unhit. Because the shot was an easy one and I didn't see how I could have missed, I hunted for him in the rocks and found him about 25 yards from where I'd last seen him. The 150-grain bullet would have killed him in his tracks.

The .30/06's 150-grain bullet is deadly on animals of the elk class if the hunter has a good broadside shot. But if the animal is in a position where the shoulder has to be broken, or a good deal of tissue penetrated, before the vital area is struck, the 180-grain is more effective.

Once I deliberately tried to break a big bull caribou's shoulder at about

170 yards with the 150-grain bullet. The bullet went to pieces in the shoulder with a noise that sounded like a firecracker going off, but it didn't even knock the bull off his feet. Most 180-grain .30/06 bullets would have gone clear through without any such shattering effect. I sent the next bullet through the upper lungs and that was the end of the caribou.

I have a .30/06 that's my pride and joy. I cherish it because it will send most any weight bullet to the same point of impact at 200 yards. The rifle weighs $9^1/_4$ pounds, with sling, Lyman Alaskan scope on a Griffin & Howe mount, and full magazine. It is built on a Fabrique Nationale (Belgian) Mauser action with a Sukalle barrel and a twist of 1 in 12 inches, and it has a superb stock by Al Biesen. When I go out for both light and heavy game, I take along 150-grain and 180-grain ammunition. The 150-grain stuff is sighted in to hit on the nose at 250 yards, the 180 at 225. At 200 yards both bullets shoot into the same group, the 150-grain bullet landing slightly higher than the 180.

When I am hunting sheep with the 150-grain stuff, and glass a grizzly, I simply shift to the 180-grain bullets and begin to stalk. I've shot six grizzlies with the 180-grain and since I haven't got eaten up by one yet, the old .30/06 must be at least adequate.

After my experience, particularly with the Remington 180-grain pointed soft-point Core-Lokt .30/06 bullet, I've concluded there's no need in America for a bullet giving greater penetration. In the Yukon I once put four of those bullets, rapid fire, right behind the shoulder of a big, rangy grizzly that measured 7 feet, 7 inches from tip of nose to tip of tail as it lay dead. The bear was on a sandbar, and every bullet fired went clear through him and cracked against rocks on the far side.

For years the favorite brown-bear medicine of Hosea Sarber, noted Alaska game warden and guide, was the 172-grain bullet of the Western Tool & Copper Works; it was loaded for a muzzle velocity of about 2,750 fps. Since Sarber felt that the load was adequate, and since he killed more grizzlies than I have ever seen, I'm going to take his word for it.

For North American hunting, the 220-grain bullet hasn't much place in the sheme of things, I believe, unless it is for Alaska brown bears. Since they're often shot at close range and in the alders, when high velocity is of no particular moment, and where the bullet would have to drive through heavy chest muscles, I can see that the 220-grain Silvertips and Core-Lokts would be the business. And if I ever hunt brownies (which I haven't so far) and carry a .30/06, those are the missiles I'll choose.

If a man wants a bullet that will go clear through a moose on a broadside shot, the 220-grain is also good; but this is hearsay on my part, for the only 220-grain .30/06 bullet I ever shot at a moose very definitely didn't go clear through, although it did break a shoulder on the way in. There's something to be said for the 220-grain in timber shooting—the heavy, round-nose bullets are deflected less by brush than a lighter bullet with sharper profile.

For the heaviest African antelope, like the eland, or for knocking over big Bengal tigers or stopping charging African lions, the 220-grain bullets make the .30/06 a real rifle. Steward Edward White used the .30/06 on dozens of lions, his bullets being the old Remington 220-grain delayed mushroom and the Western 220-grain boattail with only a pinpoint of lead exposed. He felt that for this work, the .30/06 so loaded was superior to the .405 Winchester. And yet I hear tell it's not suitable for elk!

Curiously enough, the most accurate load I ever used in a .30/06 (and one of the most accurate I've ever run across in any rifle) was the now-discontinued Western 220-grain pinpoint boattail with 52 grains of DuPont No. 4350 powder. With that load a man could shoot an elephant's eye out at 100 yards. With it I shot many groups of less than a minute of angle. In fact, I was so fascinated by its astonishing accuracy in an old Springfield of mine that I used up my small supply of bullets in group shooting.

The 220-grain bullets, because of their round noses and moderate velocity, should be the choice for elk and moose in brush and timber, since they are less likely to deflect. But under no circumstances should they be used on light game like deer, because—except for the old-fashioned soft-points, which had a lot of lead exposed—they do not open up fast enough to inflict a quick-killing wound. Few hunters would go after really heavy game, such as elephant, rhinoceros, and Cape buffalo, with a .30/06; but if it had to be done I suppose the best bet would be a full-metal-case bullet, and one has never been loaded for sporting purposes in this country.

In the past, 170-grain bullets have been loaded for the .30/06, but I can't see any great advantage in them. Likewise I don't think the 200-grain bullet is sufficiently superior to the 180-grain to pay to load it, although I used the 200-grain Barnes bullet with 56 grains of No. 4350 and found it powerful and accurate.

Long ago, for lighter game, I settled on 53 grains of the No. 4320 with the 150-grain bullet. That combination has given me good accuracy, long case life, and satisfactory killing power. And it shoots to the same point of impact as the Remington factory load with the 150-grain Bronze Point bullet. Muzzle velocity is probably about 2,825 to 2,900 fps and pressure below 50,000 pounds to the square inch.

With the 180-grain bullet, 49.5 grains of the same powder is a good bet. Likewise 56 grains of No. 4350.

For some reason most .30/06 rifles will put the 220- and 180-grain factory loads pretty much to the same point of impact at 100 yards, but they will toss the 150-grain from 5 to 7 inches higher. For that reason a .30/06 that—because of bedding or barrel contour—will lay everything pretty much to the same point of impact is one to be cherished and used sparingly.

Lads getting custom rifles made up might well specify a 1-in-12 twist, which stabilizes even the 220-grain bullets over game ranges and which will give very good accuracy with 125-grain bullets if a .30/06 owner *has* to use his rifle on varmints.

All in all, I question whether most hunters need much more rifle than the .30/06 on any North American big game. I do not think cartridge progress stopped with the .30/06 by any means, but it still is a most excellent cartridge. No doubt the .375 H&H Magnum will give more quick kills on the larger game. So will the powerful, blown-out .300 magnums like the Weatherby and .300 Winchester Magnums.

But in the .30/06 you find about all the recoil that most men can handle, and no one who is afraid of his rifle's recoil can shoot it well. It is far better to put in a well-placed shot with a .30/06 than a poorly placed shot with a shoulder-jolting .375. For the record, the recoil of a .30/06 Winchester Model 70 with the 180-grain bullet is 17 foot-pounds, whereas that of the .375 with the 300-grain bullet is almost twice as much—33.6 foot-pounds. Some riflemen claim they can shoot a .375 for fun. I can't. I believe, too, that a hunter should *enjoy* shooting his big-game rifle; if it punishes him he'll never get enough practice to become a deadly shot.

I am further convinced that reported lack of killing power in the .30/06 stems from poor shooting or unsuitable bullets—things that the finest cartridges in the world are not proof against.

Obviously, a man who shoots but one box of ammunition a year can't be a very good shot, and he wouldn't be good with any caliber. Nor can you use moose bullets on deer or woodchuck bullets on moose and expect quick kills. Use the *right* bullet for the game you hunt, practice enough so that you can place your shot accurately, and the .30/06 won't let you down.

With its moderate recoil, its readily available ammunition in a variety of bullet weights, its power, and its accuracy, the .30/06 is one of the world's great big-game cartridges.

12

The All-Around Battery

A FRIEND OF MINE with vast experience once said that no hunter would be much worse off if he confined himself to a .22 rimfire rifle, a 12-gauge shotgun, and a .30/06.

No one will deny that the .22 rimfire is the cartridge that teaches most of us to shoot, and it can also be used to collect small game for the pot. I have shot quail, doves, cottontail and jackrabbits, and squirrels with .22s. Once on a poorly planned and unsuccessful sheep hunt a companion with a Colt Woodsman .22 pistol shot a good many ruffed and blue grouse. That was all the meat we had. A very tough guy I once knew walked through snow and mountains, much of the time in zero weather, from Telegraph Creek, British Columbia, to Norman Wells, Northwest Territories. With him he had a few traps, a Hudson Bay blanket, and a Colt Woodsman automatic pistol and 300 rounds of ammunition. With the pistol he shot squirrels, porcupines, grouse, snowshoe rabbits, caribou, sheep, and moose. When he trudged into Norman Wells with several thousand dollars' worth of mink and fisher skins in his pack he was well fed and in good shape. He still had some .22 ammunition left. He had used up about half of the Hudson Bay blanket making himself socks.

In Mexico the .22 is the most widely used of cartridges. It is cheap, widely distributed, and it makes little noise. A .22 bullet in the heart, head, or spine will drop even a large animal. However, in unskillful hands it wounds a lot of game.

The 12-gauge shotgun is the world's standard. More 12-gauge shotguns are made than all others put together. Shells in 12-gauge are available wherever shotguns are used—from Austria to Zanzibar, from Australia to Zululand. Shotshells in 12 gauge are loaded with as little as 1 ounce of shot—light field loads that I use with No. 6 shot on pheasants and with No. $7^1/_2$ and No. 8 on quail and doves. They are also loaded with as much as $1^7/_8$ ounces of shot in the form of magnum loads in 3-inch cases. The standard

American 12-gauge chamber is $2^3/_4$ inches long. On the Continent such chambers are marked 70 mm. American shells are loaded heavier than European shells. In the United States more shells like Western Super-X and Remington Nitro Express are sold than any other. These are loaded with $3^3/_4$ drams equivalent of powder and $1^1/_4$ ounces of shot. The 12-gauge $2^3/_4$-inch magnums are loaded with $1^1/_2$ ounces of shot. The ordinary American 12-gauge "field" load uses $3^1/_4$ drams of powder and $1^1/_8$ ounces of shot. Most English and Continental 12-gauge guns intended for the European market have 65mm or $2^1/_2$-inch chambers. Using shells with $2^3/_4$-inch cases in such guns raises pressures somewhat and should be avoided. In fact, using maximum loads in 12-gauge $2^3/_4$-inch cases in light European guns is not advisable even if the guns have $2^3/_4$-inch chambers. Heavy loads shake light guns loose. Most British field loads use $1^1/_{16}$ ounces of shot. These are effective to use and are pleasant to shoot. I have shot grouse, Hungarian Partridge, and red-legged partridge in Europe with them

In a pinch the owner of a 12-gauge gun can use it on deer. Thousands of deer are killed each year with 12-gauge guns using buckshot or rifled slugs. With the new buckshot loads with shot protected by polyethylene "sawdust" deer can be killed quite reliably at 50 yards. With slugs in an open-bored pump or automatic 12-gauge shotgun that is correctly sighted in with either iron sights or a low-power scope, a good shot can take deer to 100 yards with rifled slugs.

At short range there is no more deadly weapon in existence than a 12-gauge shotgun loaded with buckshot. In the golden days of British East Africa (Kenya), men hunting lions used to have a 12-gauge loaded with SSg buckshot along in case a lion charged. Those who have used such guns on lions say that a cool shot who reserves his fire until the lion is 5 to 10 yards away is perfectly safe.

I have killed one deer, one coyote, and a couple of bobcats with birdshot but for the large stuff buckshot is the best.

The American rifled slug is good for deer, as they are small, thin-skinned animals. However, the slugs are actually hollow shells of pure, soft lead and do not give good penetration on large animals. They also go to pieces on brush.

Not long before I wrote these lines I read a piece by a lad who held that to do the various kinds of hunting in North America one needed, I believe, six rifles of various types and calibers. Maybe a specialized rifle like a semi-automatic in .308 or a pump in .35 Remington might have a little edge over a bolt-action .30/06 for hunting whitetails in the brush, but the advantage would not amount to very much. The first shot is the important one—and one can get off that first shot as fast with a bolt-action as he can with anything else.

I am more of an open-country hunter than I am a brush hunter. I have shot most of my deer with bolt-action rifles and cartridges like the 7 x 57, the .270, and the .30/06. But if I were buying a rifle for use only on whitetails at short range and in heavy cover it would be a Remington Model 742 semi-automatic in .308 or .280 Remington. I would fit it with a $2^1/_2$-X or possibly a 3-X scope, and sight in on the button at 100 yards. I can remember several bucks that would not have gotten away if I could have thrown in a fast second shot. The pump-action Remington and Savage are almost as fast as the automatic. The lever-action Savage, Winchester, Browning, and Marlin rifles are also faster than the bolt-actions.

The deer is not a very tough animal. If the shot is well placed anything from the .30/30 on up will do very well. Actually it might be argued that the pipsqueak .44/40 has killed more deer than any other cartridge.

The whitetail is found almost all over the United States, from Oregon to Maine, from Arizona to Montana. It is the most plentiful North American big-game animal. Some other game animals like elk and moose are a good deal larger than the whitetails and others are shot at longer ranges.

Pronghorn antelope are shot at the longest average range of any North American game animal. After reviewing my own experience I would say that most antelope are taken at 250 to 275 yards. Others are shot—and shot at—at much greater ranges. Because the antelope is an open-country animal it is seen at a distance and many hunters are tempted to blast away out of range.

The antelope hunter needs a rifle for a flat-shooting cartridge. Suitable ones are the .30/06, the .270, the .25/06, the 7mm Magnum, the 7 x 57 Mauser, the .280 Remington and the .257, .270, and 7mm Weatherby Magnums. I have done most of my antelope hunting with $2^{1}/_{2}$-X and 4-X scopes, but if I were getting a scope solely for antelope it would be a 6-X. The bolt-action is generally a bit more accurate than other types.

The antelope is a small animal. The average mature buck will field-dress 90-100 pounds and run from 14 to 16 inches from the top of the shoulder to the bottom of the brisket. The hunter should use an easily expanded bullet. I have taken more antelope with the 130-grain .270 bullet than anything else, but I have also used the 130-grain 7 x 57 bullet, the 150-grain .30/06 bullet, the 140-grain in the .275 Holland & Holland Magnum, and the 100-grain in the .257 Roberts. Soft varmint-type bullets should not be used.

The rifle should be sighted in so that at no point in the trajectory will the bullet rise more than 4 inches above the line of sight. This means about 275 yards for the .270 with the 130-grain bullet and the 7mm Magnum with the 150-grain bullet. The .30/06 with the 150-grain bullet can be sighted in for 250 yards. In any case the first shooting and sight adjustment can be done at 25 yards. Bullets should land at the point of aim, and be around 3 inches high at 100 yards.

The antelope rifle needs not be particularly light or short of barrel, as transportation in antelope country is usually by car and stalks are generally short. The rifle for saddle use and for sheep and other mountain game should be fairly light and fairly short of barrel, but not too short or too light. Around twenty years ago a gunsmith made a specialty of turning out .30/06 rifles with light 18-inch barrels. The whole rifle with scope weighed only 7 pounds. I tried one and loathed it. The thing kicked like a mule and the muzzle blast laid the daisies low.

I think the ideal rifle for scabbard and mountain use should weigh $7^{1}/_{2}$-8 pounds with scope and have a 21-22-inch barrel. My pet .270 is an old pre-1964 Winchester Model 70 Featherweight with steel trigger guard and floorplate, 22-inch barrel, Leupold 4-X scope on the now-obsolete Tilden mount, and French walnut stock by Al Biesen. It weighs 8 pounds on the button and will group good bullets into 1 inch at 100 yards. I have used it in Idaho, Wyoming, Alberta, British Columbia, the Yukon, Iran, and Botswana. With it I have shot whitetail deer, mule deer, grizzly, black bear, Dall sheep, Stone sheep, caribou, Iranian urial (wild sheep), ibex, gemsbok, greater kudu, etc. I have another .270, a post-1964 Model 70 Winchester "Mannlicher" model. The barrel is 19 inches long. It is a sweet little rifle but I'd prefer a longer barrel. The short barrel loses velocity and is a bit less steady to hold.

The Remington Model 700 in .30/06 and .270 has a 22-inch barrel and will be right on the nose for weight. The Model 700 in 7mm Remington Magnum caliber and .25/06 has a 24-inch barrel, usable but not as handy as with the shorter barrel. The Ruger Model 77 in 7 x 57, .270, and .30/06 is right on in weight and barrel length. For an all-around rifle like this I prefer a fixed-power 4-X scope.

A rifle with a barrel of much more than 22 inches is awkward to climb with, and a heavy rifle has a tendency to pull the horseback hunter's saddle to one side.

Most mountain hunting is done at least partly with horses. In sheep country, for example, the hunter will ride to the spot from which he is to make his stalk or his climb. Often elk are heard or seen at some distance and then stalked. In some types of terrain it is possible to ride until a deer or an elk is seen. Then the rider jumps off, grabs his rifle out of the scabbard, and cuts loose.

Many are the wild stories that have gone around about the incredible toughness of elk. Take it from me—with suitable bullets (most factory big-game bullets), rifles of the 7 x 57, .270 and .30/06 class are entirely adequate. Hit an elk, a moose, a caribou, or a grizzly bear through the lungs with any of them and he is not long for this world. Hit an elk in the rump or in the guts or break a leg and you are in trouble no matter what caliber you use! I have shot a dozen moose, all with the .270 except one shot with a .30/06. I have shot around twenty-five elk, seventeen with the .270, the rest with the .30/06. I have seen about as many elk and moose shot as I have shot myself. Most of the elk hit in the lungs went down in their tracks, though some ran a few yards before they fell. None of the moose fell from a lung shot but none went over 100 yards or so. I have seen moose shot with .30/06s, .270s, .300 Magnums, and .375s.

Some hunters feel happier if they hunt Alaska brown bears, polar bears, and large Alaska moose with powerful cartridges like the .300 Weatherby and the .375. I can remember when I lay in the rain on an Alaskan beach waiting for a big brown bear to walk to a piece of driftwood where I planned to let him have it. I was glad then that I was using a .375 Magnum. The polar bear is often larger than the brown, and although many have been killed with the .30/06, a .375 is by no means a bad idea. The walrus is one of the largest mammals on earth and (or so they tell me!) should be taken with a .375.

But to get back to the original proposition, there is nothing in North America and little game anywhere in the world that cannot be handled neatly with the old "workhorse" .30/06.

African hunting as it was traditionally practiced is dead. The native governments have not preserved the game. Actually some of the highest officials have been the biggest poachers. A friend who hunted in the Northern Frontier District of Kenya in January 1977 told me he saw hundreds of carcasses and skeletons of poached elephants but only three live elephants.

Be that as it may, rifles of the 7 x 57, .270, and .30/06 class do well on *all* African antelope from 15-pound dik-dik to 1,800-pound eland. My wife has shot most African game including the large antelope (kudu, roan, sable, and gemsbok) and has killed elephant and lion with .30/06 and 7 x 57 rifles.

If I were to go to Africa tomorrow I'd take a .270 and a .375. I have used the .270 in three of my eleven safaris and found it satisfactory. The .375 apparently does very well on elephants. It is fine lion medicine and an all-around useful cartridge.

But the .30/06 would do just as well as the .270, maybe for some purposes a bit better. With a .22 rimfire for small game and birds, a .30/06 for everything else from impala to elephant (with 220-grain solid bullets), and a 12-gauge the owner of the three-gun all-around battery could do very well in Africa—or anywhere else!

13

This Flinching Business

FLINCHING on the part of the shooter is supposed to be a low and discreditable business, something which nice people simply do not do, just as they don't write bum checks, take dope, or have fits. Asking a man if he has any trouble with flinching is a bit like asking him if his child has two heads or if he has poisoned the well at the orphans' home lately.

Yet many shooters always flinch. All shooters sometimes flinch—rifle shots, pistol shots, trapshooters, skeet shooters, big-game hunters. Flinching is one of the major reasons for bum shooting. Show me a man who can honestly say he has never flinched and I'll show you a man who has never shot a gun.

Sad thing about it is that many a citizen is convinced that he holds like a rock and that he never flinches. This is one of the major reasons why some people shoot forever and never get any better, why some cannot successfully call their shots.

What a good flinch can do to an otherwise properly held shot is wonderful to behold. Results are most marked with a handgun with its light weight and short barrel, but flinching with a rifle can throw a shot wide and I am convinced that a nice well-executed flinch can even cause a miss with a wide-patterning shotgun.

I write this piece as an authority, by the way, as I have flinched with every sort of an instrument that burns powder and some that don't. I am free to admit it.

Sad thing about flinching, as I have said, is that most of its practitioners have no notion that they flinch. If they do not realize it, they cannot cure it.

First, what causes a flinch? The usual explanation is that flinching is caused by the fear of recoil—of getting hurt by the bump and scared by the muzzle blast and report. Our boy knows that when the gun goes off he is going to be bumped and socked and that his ears are going to ring. So, he cringes (flinches) just as he finishes his trigger pull and knows he is bringing about these bad and unpleasant things.

This explanation is partly or even largely true, but flinching is also caused by nervous tension. I have seen men who almost never flinched in rifle practice but who always flinched in a match and whose scores went down accordingly. I have seen others who never flinched when shooting at a tin can yet who would flinch when trying to pop at a rabbit.

A pal of mine who is a very good skeet shot was, some years ago, just about to break his first 25 straight, something to which he had looked forward for months. He got past all his tough singles without a miss, broke the doubles at Stations 1, 2 and 6. Knowing he had it made, he began to sweat. He called for the doubles at station 7, broke them both. All that was left was his optional target. He stood in his tracks, wiped the sweat from his brow, called for the low-house bird, which there at Station 7 goes straight away. It is a genuinely easy shot. But did the lad break it? He did not! Instead he closed his eyes, gave a heck of a flinch, and missed it.

First step in curing this very common habit of flinching is for the shooter to realize and admit that he flinches. Until he does that his case is as hopeless as that of a man suffering from some undiagnosed physical ailment.

How do you find out?

Simple! Have a pal load and cock a gun and hand it to you to shoot, sometimes leaving the chamber empty and sometimes not. If you flinch you'll find yourself contracting the muscles of the shoulder, jerking the trigger of the empty gun. When the gun is loaded, the recoil covers the flinch; but when empty, it doesn't.

Not long ago a young man who had been away to college and who had not shot a high-powered rifle for some months was out with me. He sat down, took a pop at a stone with a diameter of about 1 foot, and about 200 yards away. He missed it, took another shot, and missed it the second time.

"You're flinching," I told him.

"I am not either," he said, insulted.

I took the rifle, pretended to load it, but instead handed it back with an empty chamber, and told him to take another pop at the rock. As the firing pin clicked down he jumped a foot. Grinning sheepishly, he admitted he had been flinching. I took the rifle again, but this time I eased a cartridge into the chamber.

"All right," I said. "You know the chamber is empty this time so squeeze her off with those crosshairs right in the middle of the rock." He did and white powder flew right from the center. Convinced that he had been flinching, he shot well from then on.

This was quick detection and quick cure, but the boy had fought his battles with flinching before.

Once a man realizes that he flinches, he has two ways of curing it. The first—and the one which is recommended by the army—is for the marksman to squeeze the trigger so gradually that he does not know when the gun is going off. When the sights look right the pressure on the trigger is increased a bit, when the sights swing off, the pressure is held. When the gun goes off, the report and muzzle blast will come as a surprise and our hero won't have time to flinch. This method is sometimes called "surprise

A high-powered rifle, such as a .416 Rigby, can "slug" a shooter with recoil that can lift his elbows off his knees. The best way to hit with heavy artillery like this is to apply pressure on the trigger very gradually with no tendency to yank, concentrating on trigger squeeze, sight alignment, and target, and not on what's going to happen when the gun goes off.

fire" and a very good method it is. The beginner should always be instructed to hold and squeeze them that way, and he should always begin either from a rest of some sort or from prone because then his rifle is comparatively steady and he does not have the temptation to make a grab at his trigger to catch a bull's-eye as it goes by.

Some old and experienced and also very fine shots claim they always use this surprise-fire method of shooting anything and from any position. Others claim they always know when the gun is going off.

My own first love is the rifle. I am a rather fair rifle shot and not too bad with a shotgun. I know about when both are going off. But there is only one way I can shoot a handgun and keep from flinching and that is to hold as well as I can and squeeze off by the surprise-fire method. If I try to catch the bulls as they go by, I flinch—doggone it, I flinch!

Shooting offhand with a rifle, which is sort of a sister of handgun shooting, I have very little tendency to flinch, as shown by the fact that when I was doing a good deal of offhand shooting I almost never got one out of the 4-ring. *But* I have noticed that if I have difficulty in getting a shot off and take so long that my muscles get tired I sometimes flinch and throw a wild one. The idea seems to be that my muscles say they are tired so let's yank it off and get it over with. The remedy for that is to put the doggoned cannon down and rest the arms.

We have seen that one way to cure the flinch is to attempt to kid yourself and squeeze off so gradually you will not know when the gun is going off. The other way to cure it is by conscious exercise of the will, *by concentration on target and sight alignment instead of what's going to happen at the butt end.*

Target shots do a lot of snickering at characters who claim they can shoot better at game than at targets. For the most part these lads are kidding themselves, but there is enough to it to lend some truth to the statement. What they are saying is actually this: That when they are shooting at game they concentrate on their sights and what they want to hit and temporarily forget the blast and kick of the rifle. Gal I know who has killed a lot of African game with a .465 Nitro Express which turns up about 60 foot-pounds of free recoil tells me that she never even feels the recoil and practically doesn't hear that cannon go off when she is taking a pop at a rhino, an elephant, or a bad-tempered lion. Others who shoot .375 Magnums tell me they never notice recoil when shooting at game and presumably they do not flinch.

Every good or even fairly good shot calls every single shot—with rifle, shotgun or handgun. If the target shooter lets off his shot with the intersection of crosshairs hanging right in the middle of the bull, but gets a wide 4 at 1:30 instead, if the trap shooter swings up and gets a bit ahead of his quartering target, swears the thing should have broken when it didn't, if the big game hunter swears he could see the reticule of his scope right on that monster buck at a scant 100 yards and yet missed him, if the handgun shooter declares he got that one off with a perfect sight picture and yet got a lousy 7 . . . the answer in every case is a flinch.

When a man *knows* he flinches and resolves to cure himself the battle is half won. Probably the best answer in the way of a cure is a combination of the two recommended methods. First he can train himself to apply the pressure on the trigger very gradually with no tendency to yank, concentrating on trigger squeeze, sight alignment, and target, and *not* on what's going to happen when the gun goes off. Second, he can train himself *not* to flinch by conscious desire not to, and by making it a point to follow through on his shot, to try to keep his sights aligned *after the trigger falls*. This business of letting go all holds when the trigger falls is highly conducive to flinching.

Our boy also makes this business of curing or not developing a flinch much easier if he doesn't overgun himself. Some people have much greater recoil tolerance than others. The average trained shot can shoot a .270 or .30/06 without much flinching trouble, but few can shoot a rifle of heavier recoil without jumping now and then. Most people, though, are afraid to admit that they are recoil-sensitive, apparently feeling that if they did they would be admitting they were sissies.

I can usually sit down with a .375 Magnum and keep all or nearly all of the first five shots in a 10-inch bull at 200 yards. If I fire another string immediately after, my score drops off. Why? I flinch. No one should hunt with a rifle he is afraid of. He'll shoot better and kill cleaner with a rifle which is within his recoil tolerance and which will not cause him to flinch. A perfectly placed shot with a .30/30 is more deadly than a poorly placed shot with a .375 Magnum, and don't let anyone tell you differently.

There is nothing disgraceful about flinching, then. It is done in the best families and by the best shots, but no one can cure a flinch unless he *knows* *he flinches.* When he realizes that, he can go about a cure by adopting a gradual trigger squeeze, by putting the kick and muzzle blast out of his mind

If you have to shoot offhand in the field, keep your right elbow up and your left elbow under the fore-end.

and by concentrating on the sight picture and the follow-through. He can help matters by not overgunning himself.

The man who makes up his mind that he isn't going to flinch and who then applies his pressure on the trigger so gradually that it slips off an ounce at a time and who does his damnedest to keep his sight aligned after the firing pin falls isn't going to have time to do much flinching!

USE THE SEAT OF YOUR PANTS

On the plains and in the mountains, the sitting position is the most useful of them all when you're after big game. It isn't quite as steady as the prone, so your shooting will be a little less accurate, It isn't quite as fast as the offhand when you have an easy-to-hit target, but it's a lot faster for a *precise* shot at a difficult mark. It doesn't put the line of sight quite as high above the ground as the kneeling position, but it's a heck of a lot steadier. Finally, it can be used under a greater variety of conditions than any other reasonably steady position.

Of the big game I have shot, I'd estimate that I have killed about 70 percent from the sit, about 20 percent offhand, and 5 percent each kneeling and prone.

I do about three-fourths of my practicing from the sitting position, the rest offhand. I use the kneeling position very rarely, and my prone position is usually not the conventional type—I rest the rifle's forearm on a rolled-up jacket placed on a stone, a log, or something of the sort.

In the mountain and canyon country of the Southwest, where I grew up, the usual shots at deer are across canyons that may be from 150 to 400 yards wide. When game pops into view, the thing to do is to sit down instantly, get on, and touch her off. But *sit!* Once I sat down and got off a shot so quickly at a running buck that my companion, who was looking the other way and didn't see the deer, thought the gun had gone off accidentally. From my first sight of the deer until it lay dead three seconds may have elapsed.

On the other hand I remember taking an offhand shot at a buck drowsing under a tree like a sleepy horse. I was in waist-high chaparral and, of course, could not have seen him if I sat down. The buck was between 250 and 300 yards away. I assumed my best target stance but my sights wavered all over the buck and 20 or 30 feet of the surrounding territory. It must have taken me a good minute to get off the shot. If I had been able to sit down I could have knocked off that buck within seconds.

When I used to shoot a lot of running antelope and blacktail jackrabbits, I'd sit down if the target was much more than 100 yards away. Sitting is not as flexible as the offhand or even the kneeling position, but it is flexible enough to cope with most running game in open country. Its major hazard is that you may sit on something that wasn't meant to be sat on, but that seems of small consequence when a buck mule deer with 10 points and a 38-inch spread is on the opposite side of the canyon.

I have carried home many a bruise from sharp rocks or sticks, but my worst punishment came, not when I was after a lordly buck, but when I ran into a whole flock of jackrabbits. I came over a ridge and there, on the opposite side, were five or six big juicy antelope jacks. Automatically I went into a sit—on a pile of cholla balls. Imagine about 10,000 No. 10 fishhooks sticking out of an egg and you have it. I had 7,692 cactus thorns in my rear end and I slept on my stomach for a week.

The sitting position is not only fast and fairly steady but, best of all, it can be used—unlike prone or kneeling—to shoot across or down a hillside. For mountain hunting it is the business. In plains hunting it is very useful for a steady shot when no rest is available and you can't lie prone because grass and weeds are too high or because cactus, thorns, or sharp rocks make lying down hazardous.

Just how accurately can a lightweight, scope-sighted hunting rifle be shot from the sit? A good rifleman should be able to keep three-fourths of his shots inside a 10-inch bull at 300 yards. Now and then he'll score a possible, but ordinarily from one to three or four shots will wander out of the black. They should not, however, be *far* out.

Holding an 8- or $9^1/_2$-pound hunting rifle steady is harder than holding down a $10^1/_2$ or $11^1/_2$-pound target rifle. At 200 yards, if our boy is holding and squeezing well, practically *all* the shots should be pretty well centered in the 10-inch black. On occasion I've shot such groups running around 4 inches. And once, with a scope-sighted .270, I grouped five shots at 200 yards that measured only about $2^3/_4$ inches across. But I don't kid myself that in these cases it wasn't about 85 percent luck.

Be that as it may, a good shot with a 4-X scope on an accurate rifle will kill more jackrabbits and woodchucks at 200 yards from the sit than he'll miss. And even at 300 yards with a scope of 8-X or 10-X, he'll make a surprising proportion of one-shot kills. Since errors of aim from the sitting position tend to be horizontal rather than vertical, there is more leeway on a big-game animal than on a varmint, so it's no astounding feat to place all shots in the forward half of an elk or caribou at 400 yards.

In shooting game—be it jackrabbit, woodchuck, whitetail deer, grizzly bear, or what have you—there are no close 4s. Only the 5s count. It is bet-ter by far to get in one well-aimed, well-held, well-placed shot from the sit than to get in three or four poorly aimed, poorly held, poorly placed shots or misses offhand. No time to sit? I have seen many a man miss three or four shots at standing game that he could have killed dead if he'd taken a second to plant his posterior on the earth.

Recently I read about an African lion hunter who, when faced with a charge, always sat down if the grass was not too high. He figured on getting off one well-held, well-aimed shot and knocking the lion for a loop.

When the uninstructed beginner first tries the sitting position, he almost always makes one principal mistake, He sits up too straight and puts his wobbly elbows right on his wobbly kneecaps. That position is little steadier, if any, than offhand. The secret of a good sitting position is to lean forward and put the flat of the left arm, just above the elbow, against the flat of the shin just below the left knee. Feet should be well apart and feet and ankles relaxed. I have often read that the heels should be dug into the ground. That's the poorest advice I know of, since the digging induces a tremor. The only time the rifleman should jam his heels into the ground is when he's shooting from a steep hillside and has to dig in to keep from skidding.

Everyone, I believe, has to work out the minor details of his own sitting position for himself. A man with a paunch, for instance, cannot bend forward as far as a flat-bellied youth. Some riflemen prefer crossed legs rather than outstretched ones. For me, though, the key to a good solid sit-ting position is the relationship of left arm and shin, as described above. What happens to the right arm is relatively unimportant, just so the posi-tion feels comfortable and *relaxed*. The natural tension of the back muscles will pull the upper arms against the shin and bring equilibrium and relative steadiness.

In no position should a rifleman try to hold by main strength. He should always feel relaxed. The harder a man tries to hold, the more tense he becomes; and the more tension, the greater the wobble.

My own besetting sin is tenseness. I often catch myself bearing down, de-termined to hold that damned rifle steady if I have to squeeze it in two at the grip—and when I hold like that the old musket wobbles all over the target. Then I must *deliberately* loosen up.

I am convinced that the difference between the ordinary good rifleman and the superlative one is not that the latter has better eyes or muscles, or is smarter or better-looking, but simply that he can relax, even when picking off the biggest buck he ever saw at 350 yards or firing the last shot in a string when a 5 will mean a win and a 4 a tie. The more relaxed the rifle shot is, the steadier he tends to be and the more he can concentrate on a gentle trigger squeeze.

If a man misses a standing buck from the sitting position up to 250 yards,

Jack Slack, crack rifle shot and Leupold Stevens sales and advertising manager, uses a tight sling in an improvised position on a varmint shoot.

it's not because he couldn't hold properly but because he yanked his shot. Really wild shots always come from a yank. Sometimes, of course, a shot may "get away" from a shooter; that's because the rifle goes off when the squeeze is in progress but not at the precise moment the shooter wants it to. Such a shot hits out of the black on the target range, or out of the vital area on game, but the deviation won't be very wide. The lad who misses his game by feet or who knocks out 3s and 2s on a target or misses it completely does so *not* because he cannot hold steady but because he is yanking the trigger. Under any conditions, it must always be squeezed gently. A good rifleman may squeeze it *fast,* but he squeezes it, never yanks it!

Years ago another citizen and I were doing some revolver shooting. I was pretty sour. I protested that I couldn't hold the lousy roscoe steady. "That's not the trouble," quoth my companion. "You're yanking the trigger, trying to catch the 10s as they go by. You can't shoot a handgun like that. You're jerking the whole thing."

Then he demonstrated. He took the revolver and deliberately wobbled it far more than even the poorest holder would. *But he squeezed his shots off.* He didn't get all of them in the black by any means, but he had no wild shots such as I'd been getting. I learned my lesson then and there.

A good gunsling, properly adjusted, is one of the great inventions of the human race, along with fire and the wheel. Particularly wonderful is it to the sitting rifleman who wants to polish off a woodchuck perched insolently on a rock at 200 yards, or to nail a fine buck poised for flight, high on some lofty ridge way out yonder. Every game shot who takes his shooting seriously owes it to himself to get a good sling, then learn how to adjust it and use it. And never forget that a sling takes the curse off toting a heavy rifle, which otherwise is one of the most awkward burdens known to man. You couldn't run fast enough to present me with a rifle to which a sling could not be attached, even if said rifle were done up in $20 bills.

Best type of sling for the hunter is the one-piece Whelen type, $7/8$ inch wide. It's much better for our purposes than the $1^1/_4$-inch two-piece military and target sling. Normally, the front swivel should be about 15 inches forward of the center of the trigger. Short-armed men want it farther back, and target shooters who use a low prone position want it farther forward. That's why swivels on target arms are adjustable for position.

The sling can be permanently adjusted for use in the sitting position and for carrying. The one-piece sling is a single strip of leather 52 inches long, with a claw hook at one end; holes are punched into the strap to take the hook. The sling also has two keepers and a stout leather lacing.

Except for prone with tight sling, or prone with the fore-end of the rifle resting on some object, the sitting position is the steadiest and the easiest to shoot accurately from. The rough-and-ready "practical" hunter should not sneer at it as belonging only on the target range. It's a wonderfully effective position for the game shot, one that enables him to place his bullets humanely on big game and to knock off varmints at long ranges when he cannot lie prone.

The sitting position, then, is one to cultivate, both with and without sling, if you aspire to be a good game shot. If you practice it, you'll be rewarded by shots that will warm your heart and by trophies you couldn't otherwise have got.

It's the ace of the hunting positions!

14

Where to Hit 'Em

OVER THE YEARS my conviction has grown that it's hard to overemphasize the importance of shot placement. Poorly placed shots may sometimes kill animals that weighed anywhere from 35 to 150 pounds field-dressed, but for larger animals bullets have to be laid in there with a good deal of precision or the hunter will find himself in trouble.

Even small animals when poorly hit sometimes seem indestructible. I once saw an Arizona whitetail deer that weighed about 100 pounds field-dressed absorb fourteen bullets from a .348 Winchester, a .30/06, and a .257 before it went down. The little Thomson's gazelle of Africa dresses out at about 35 pounds; I hit one too far back with a 180-grain .300 Magnum bullet and over 3,000 foot-pounds of energy, and had to use a second shot.

It's true that if a missile has enough energy and destroys enough tissue, most any animal can be killed with a hit almost anywhere. The varmint hunter, for instance, can blow a woodchuck to kingdom come with an abdominal hit from a .220 Swift. And hitting running coyotes back of the diaphragm with 100- and 130-grain .270 bullets, I've made instant kills.

With the same bullets and poorly placed shots I have also killed Arizona whitetail deer that would dress out at say 100 pounds. A small deer, hit solidly with a fast-stepping quick-opening bullet—like a good 130-grain .270, 139-grain 7 x 57, or 150-grain .30/06 or .300 Magnum—is usually stunned and disabled even if he is not killed.

But larger animals are usually tough to kill quickly with anything except a well-placed shot. People don't pop elk just anywhere, then walk over, pick them up, and put them in their pockets. Or moose. Or grizzly bears. Or African lions!

The reason isn't difficult to find.

A 130-grain .270 bullet at a muzzle velocity of 3,140 fps and turning up a retained energy of 1,920 foot-pounds at 200 yards will usually knock the socks off of a 100-pound animal. The average elk with his insides out will weigh five or six times that much. But do we hit him with five or six times as much energy as the .270 delivers at 200 yards? We do not! If we bop him with the 270-grain bullet from a .375 Magnum at the same distance we have hit him with only a bit over 50 percent more energy—or 2,920 foot-pounds' worth. If we could jump our energy 500 or 600 percent we could kill or disable our elk with the same sloppy hits that will bowl over small deer and antelope.

We could do the same thing for moose if we could increase that energy ten or twelve times. But we can't; a weapon with ten times more energy than the .270 or the .30/06 puts out would be in the nature of an aircraft cannon. The great loads used in heavy British double rifles on the world's largest, toughest, and most dangerous game average in muzzle energy only about 5,000 foot-pounds, or less than twice that turned up by rifles of the .270—.30/06 class. To be specific, the .470 Nitro Express, which is the most popular of all African elephant cartridges, drives a 500-grain bullet at a muzzle velocity of 2,125 fps and a muzzle energy of 5,030 foot-pounds.

Or take the tremendous .50 caliber machine-gun cartridge used by the U.S. Army and Air Force. Driving its 761-grain bullet at a muzzle velocity of about 2,550 fps, with well over 10,000 foot-pounds of energy, it makes the .470 look puny. Still it is less than four times as powerful as the common or garden .30/06.

Now on rare occasions an elk may field-dress as much as 800 pounds, and a moose of the far north as much as 1,200 or 1,400 pounds. The Alaska brown bear is another big fellow and much more tenacious of life than a moose. The Cape buffalo of Africa weighs over a ton, the rhino a ton and a half, while the gargantuan elephant makes even a rhino look small.

I know of two pieces of shooting equipment that would make a fortune for anyone who could invent them. One is a shotgun sight which by some hocus-pocus would make proper lead in wing-shooting so simple that any duffer could without toil or trouble become a crack scattergunner. The other is a big-game cartridge so potent that an animal clipped anywhere with the bullet would fall dead instantly. At one extreme the ultra-high-velocity fans dream of tiny bullets at velocities of 8,000 to 10,000 fps that will salivate anything that walks, no matter where hit. Equally utopian are the boys who think all they need is a bullet large enough and heavy enough so that they can hit an animal almost anywhere and he'll give up the ghost.

I'll admit that these dreams are seductive but I think that they'll always remain dreams. For a long, long time—as long as powder and bullets are anything like those we shoot today—we'll have to try for well-placed shots.

The principal thing to remember is that an animal *lives* in the forward two-fifths of his body. The organs necessary for life are there, forward of the diaphragm. If an animal's heart does not beat, or if his lungs do not send oxygen to his brain, he quickly dies. The organs of assimilation which we colloquially call guts are not immediately necessary for life. One time I saw a bighorn ram which a companion had shot run several hundreds yards without entrails. Many people lead useful lives without stomachs and the world is full of those who've lost considerable intestine. Terror-stricken animals with broken legs seem able to travel forever, and all of us know people who have one leg or none.

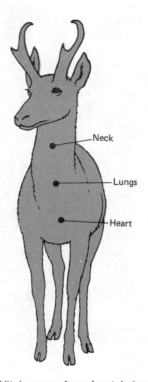

Vital organs from frontal view

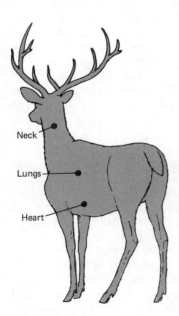

Aiming points when animal is quartering away.

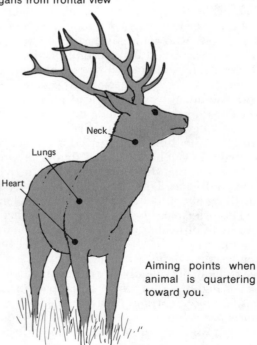

Aiming points when animal is quartering toward you.

On the other hand, death comes quickly if much damage is done in the heart-lung area. A relatively puny bullet through the lungs will cause enough hemorrhage in a short time to kill even very large animals. Karamojo Bell, who shot over 1,000 elephants with a 7 x 57 mm Mauser, used to drive the little 175-grain full-metal-case (solid) bullet into the lungs of the great beasts at night (when he could not see well enough to make his favorite brain shot), then listen carefully so that he'd hear them crash to the ground when their lungs filled up with blood. A .30/30 bullet through the lungs of an elk, or even a moose, will kill him in a short time because he'll bleed to death internally. The bullets of a .30/06 or a .270 will kill faster because they tear up more lung, do more damage.

Perhaps because it also disrupts the nerves leading to the heart and brain, a high-velocity bullet through the lungs often brings instant death. A few inches' difference in placement can be of enormous importance. Once, when the limit on sheep in British Columbia north of the Edmonton–Prince Rupert railway was two instead of one, I shot two superb rams from the same spot with a .270. The first ram was standing on a point about 200 yards away. The bullet struck his lungs and he was killed instantly in his tracks. The other ram was farther away than I thought and the bullets were falling low, hitting the brisket instead of heart or lungs. The first shot, which went in at an angle low behind his right leg, almost took his left leg off and anchored him; but I fired a fourth shot before he went down.

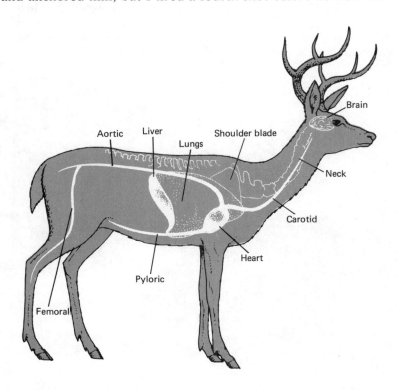

Hit solidly in the lung area with a well-designed bullet of adequate weight, caliber, and impact velocity, any animal is quickly killed. Hit anywhere else except brain or spine, he may or may not be. Various suggestions have been given as to the proper way to reach the lungs. One famous piece of advice is to follow the front leg up one-third of the way into the body with the sight, then to touch off the shot. Another is to aim to break the shoulder on the animal's far side.

On a nondangerous game animal I always try to land my shot in the lung area. It is the best shot I know of. The target is large, easy to hit, and while a bullet in that spot is fatal it destroys no meat that is ordinarily eaten. Plan to hit well forward and about halfway between backbone and brisket, and you'll have a good deal of leeway. If the bullet lands high it will break the spine or cause paralysis by striking important nerves. If far forward it may break the shoulders, if low it may strike the heart.

I am not mad about heart shots, particularly on dangerous game, because a heart-shot animal can run from 40 to 150 yards or more and still have enough vitality to take a bite out of the hunter. Actually it is typical for the heart-shot animal to take off on a wild run, then fall dead.

I don't like neck shots under ordinary circumstances either. Unless the spine is broken a neck shot is not fatal. I once tried to break the neck of a topi (a handsome African antelope that weighs about 350 pounds) with a .375. The bullet missed the spine, but knocked the topi out. The boys ran in to cut his throat and make him fit for Mohammedans to eat. Then when they got the throat cut the topi jumped up and ran off for 100 yards.

Nor do I like head shots ordinarily. It is too easy to miss the brain and maim an animal so it will die even though it gets away.

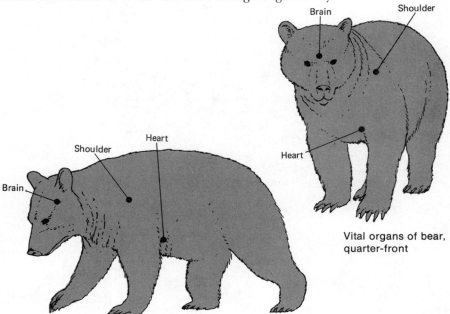

Vital organs of bear, quarter-front

Vital organs of bear, side view

Best place to hit a potentially dangerous animal like an African lion, a leopard, or a brown or grizzly bear is through both shoulders. Then with his means of locomotion broken down he can't come frisking over to eat you up. White hunters tell me that the way to thwart a charging rhino is to bust him through the shoulder you can see. That spills him.

No matter what position the nondangerous animal is in, the bullet should be driven toward the large and vulnerable heart-lung area. If a beast is facing the hunter, aim should be taken from one-third to one-half the way up the chest. If he is quartering away, it is wise to try to drive the bullet through the lungs toward the far shoulder. If he is running directly away, a shot at the root of the tail will bring an animal down with paralyzed hindquarters. A bullet that strikes a bit lower and between the hams will encounter little resistance and will often reach the lungs.

I believe I shot the first head of big game ever killed with the Remington 130-grain Bronze-point .270 bullet. This was literally years before the bullet came out commercially. A whitetail buck was running directly away from me at about 275–300 yards when the bullet hit him. He piled up stone dead and we dug the bullet out from under the skin by his right shoulder. Darned buck didn't have a bullet hole in him!

I am not going to confuse my gentle readers with a lot of anatomy. After all, they are hunters and not surgeons going in after gallstones. If they keep those bullets up front they'll be hitting the animal where he lives—and they won't have to brood too much about what they hit him with.

But, you ask, what about those shots at an antelope running with the throttle open, at a mule deer going up the opposite side of a canyon 200 yards or more away, or at a whitetail buck leaping over a windfall? Are you supposed to pass those shots up?

Not necessarily. Anyone who's done much big-game hunting knows there are occasions when a hit anywhere is a pretty darned good shot. The thing to do then is to use a rifle with as much soup as you can manage—a .270, a .30/06, even a .300 Magnum on those running antelope and bounding mule deer at long range, a .30/06, a .300 Savage, or a .348 at those jumping whitetails. If you must shoot at the hind end of an elk in timber, even the .375 Magnum is not too heavy.

But ordinarily, if you have the skill and temperament to place your shot in the vital lung area, to break the shoulders, or to sever the spinal cord, you can get by with a relatively light rifle.

15

Hitting Game at Long Range

A GOOD DEAL OF MOONSHINE has been written about shooting big game at long range. On one hand we have the boys of limited experience—most of it acquired in brush and forest—who say that anyone who claims to have knocked off a deer at over 150 yards is a liar. They haven't done it, and they haven't seen it done, so they won't believe anyone does it. At the other extreme are the imaginative citizens who never kill a head of game at less than 300 yards and find a 500-yard shot just routine.

For my part, I prefer a sensible median between trying to shoot an animal across a township and getting close enough to ram the rifle muzzle down its throat. Most astute procedure is to do execution at from 75 to 150 yards, if circumstances permit. Usually it isn't difficult to stalk to such a distance, but the closer one gets to the game the more chance there is of disturbing it. At 100–150 yards a rifleman worthy of the name should be able to place his bullet within from 2 to 3 inches of where he holds, and he can kill as well as if he were within 50 feet. At that distance, the hunter is not nearly so liable to get grizzly fever as he would if close enough to hit the bear with a rock.

If I were a guide and had a dude out who even looked as if he wanted to shoot a grizzly at 500 yards, I'd wrap his rifle around his neck. Anyone who hunts dangerous game—be it grizzlies or Alaska brown bears in North America, or buffaloes, lions, or leopards on the African plains—has no business taking long-range shots. Promiscuous long-range shooting by gents without judgment results in too many wounded animals getting away, and in the case of dangerous game, too much chance somebody will have his leg chewed off.

Legitimate shooting at long range requires, first of all , the rather poorly distributed commodity called judgment, something which many of us, alas, do not have. Before a rifleman takes a pop at an animal beyond his sure hitting range, he should pause and ask himself what will happen if he wounds the beast. Once I was riding back toward camp with a trigger-happy character when we saw a big bull moose, with enormous snowy-white antlers, standing on the far side of a muskeg meadow. He was about 400 yards away and right at the edge of heavy timber. This citizen jumped off his horse and before you could say "glockenspiel" he had fired offhand. I heard the plunk of the bullet on a water-filled stomach, and the bull faded into the timber. We found no blood, but we did find some hairs cut off by the bullet. We tracked the bull about a quarter of a mile but it grew dark back in the timber and we had to return to our horses and ride to camp. As far as I could see, our boy suffered no remorse. But all he'd done was donate some meat to the wolves.

That was no time for a long-range shot. Here's why: 1. The hunter couldn't get into a steady position. 2. A moose is a big, tough animal that is very difficult to kill at 400 yards with a .30/06—or with any weapon short of a 37mm cannon. 3. The bull was standing at the edge of the timber and would be out of sight in one jump. 4. Only a few minutes of light remained.

But if our hunter had caught the bull in an open basin above timberline where it couldn't get out of sight until he had a chance for a dozen shots, *and* if he were then able to get into a steady position, *and* if he were desperate for a moose trophy, he might have been justified in taking a chance on a long shot.

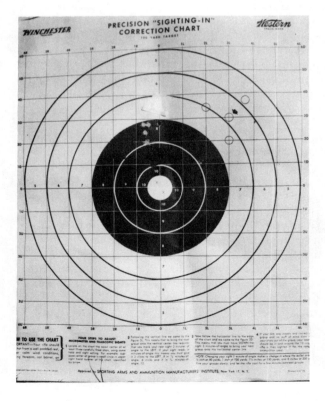

If your big-game rifle is correctly sighted in for long range, this is about what you should expect at 100 yards—a group 2$\frac{1}{2}$ to 3 inches high.

Just what is a long-range shot on big game? Defined conservatively, it is any shot made beyond the ordinary point-blank range of the rifle in use. And that means any shot in which the bullet will fall more than 4 inches below the line of sight and where allowance for drop is necessary.

Take an iron-sighted rifle of the .30/30 class sighted in to put the bullet at point of aim at 150 yards (which is the usual practice). With such a rifle, any range beyond about 190 yards (at which point the bullet has dropped 4 inches) can be considered long range. With a scope-sighted .30/06 using the 180-grain bullet and sighted in to hit the point of aim at 200 yards anything over 250 yards is long range. With a .30/06 sighted for 250 yards with the 150-grain bullet, anything beyond about 290 yards is long range—and the same figures apply to the .300 Magnum with the 180-grain bullet.

With a .270, scope-sighted for 275 yards, anything beyond 325 is long range. Big-game rifles of still higher velocity—like the Weatherby series of .270, 7mm, and .300 Magnum—have a still longer point-blank range. In their case the critical point—the 4-inch bullet drop—is about at 350 yards, or farther than with the standard .270.

And let's remember that even with the flat-shooting .300 Weatherby Magnum at 350 yards, a shot is a good one if it lands in the chest cavity; after all, the human being behind the rifle is still a human being, with human tremors and shakes and wobbles.

Great aids to long-range shooting are a flat-shooting, accurate rifle and a scope of good definition (so the rifleman can see exactly where he is holding). Then the combination should be sighted in for the longest possible point-blank range, so that the rise of the bullet above the line of sight will not cause midrange misses. That means, if the target is a big-game animal, that the bullet should not rise more than 4 inches—possibly 5—above the line of sight. The less guessing about holdover a man has to do, the better off he is. Even the most experienced and skillful riflemen lay plenty of eggs. That is why—if there is any possibility at all of a shot at longer than usual range—a hunter is a sucker to sight in a .30/30 for 100 yards or a .270 or .30/06 for 200.

It's much wiser, if a long-range shot is likely to present itself, to sight in for the longest possible range and to use a scope of good definition. A 4-X is a fine compromise for this "if" sort of hunting. For open-country shooting exclusively—when a shot at under 150 yards is the exception—a lot of very shrewd riflemen are going to the 6-X scopes.

The importance of sighting in for the longest possible range was impressed on me many years ago, when I did a lot of hunting for the smart and elusive little Arizona whitetail deer in southern Arizona and northern Sonora, Mexico. Most of my shots were from hillside to hillside or across canyons at longish and undetermined range. I found I could hit the whitetails better with a .270 than with a .30/06 because of the former's somewhat higher velocity and flatter trajectory; better with a .270 sighted for 275 or 300 yards than with one sighted in for 200; and better with a 4-X scope than with a 2½-X. The reason? When a buck bounces out across the canyon, my instinct (and I believe everyone's instinct) is to blast away directly at him instead of figuring the angles and holding over.

Some experienced long-range shooters use a rope loop to steady knees in sitting position. Just hang it over your knees for a quick sitting position.

It is usually possible to get close to many animals, particularly in open mountains where they can be located and stalked by a concealed approach from behind a ridge. But some have to be taken at long range. Those little Arizona whitetails are an example. Mule deer in many sections are found in open country, where frequently they cannot be approached, and antelope are almost always open-country game. In many cases it is the better part of wisdom for the hunter to take a long shot at a standing animal than to attempt to get closer, sometimes not much closer, and have to take the risk of a running shot.

In broken-up country, antelope—like wild sheep—can be closely approached. But if the country is flat and open, or even gently rolling—with the top of one little rise half a mile or more from another—antelope are a long-range proposition. In some areas the hunter will see ten elk at 300–400 yards for every one he sees at lesser range. If he is going to fill the home freezer he is going to have to do some long-range shooting. Much of Idaho's Selway country is like that—great brushy ridges cut by enormous canyons.

Judgment of range is by no means easy. Animals look closer in good light than in poor, farther away when seen from above or below than when seen on the level. They look closer across a canyon with no intervening objects, closer across a perfectly flat, level plain with no vegetation.

Now and then a hunter runs into a guide who is an expert rifle shot and a good judge of range. Such a guide is well worth listening to. But many guides, while they've killed a lot of big game, have done it only at short range. Often they are not expert riflemen or particularly good judges of range. Because of these factors, they chronically overestimate range, and to many anything over 150 yards is 400 yards. I once killed a ram that my guide swore was "over a quarter of a mile away." I held dead on with the .270 and hit about where I held. The ram was probably about 250–275 yards from the muzzle. An antelope that a guide swore was 500 or 600 yards away was likewise killed with a dead-on hold, and the range was no more than 300 yards.

There are two methods of arriving at a fair estimate of range. One, if the terrain permits, is to divide the intervening country with your eye into 100-yard units. Of course, that calls for out-of-season practice over measured terrain. Golfers, with their trained eyes, are usually very good at guessing hunting ranges. The other is to use some sort of a rangefinding scope reticule in comparison with the depth of the animal's chest.

Sad to say, both methods are only approximate, but they do save the rifleman from extremely bad errors. If game animals came in standard sizes, the rangefinder reticule would be quite efficient, but alas, they do not. Deer run from 14 to 20 inches from top of shoulder to bottom of brisket; adult antelope 14 to 16; a big ram or a goat from 20 to 22; an elk from 24 to 28; a bull moose from 30 to 40, with 36 being about the average of those I have measured; a coyote 8 or 9.

A rangefinder reticule consisting of two horizontal crosswires is available in some scopes. The space between the wires subtends 6 minutes of angle. If the chest area of a full-grown deer fills that space, you can estimate that he is around 300 yards away. I have also used a 4-minute Lee dot in a $2^1/_2$-X scope and found it very useful; often it prevented very poor snap judgment.

The usual long-range shot is from 300 to 450 yards at a standing and undisturbed animal. Actually it is easier to make a neat, clean kill from a good rest on a stationary target at long range than it is to make one from the offhand position at 200 yards.

For real long-range shooting, the hunter should get into the steadiest position possible. Now and then the terrain permits him to shoot prone with a tight sling, but that's quite rare in big-game hunting. The long-range big-game shot faces exactly the same problem as the varmint hunter who likes to knock off chucks at from 300 to 400 yards and he should follow his example of using a rifle rest at every opportunity. Few people can hold steady enough, even from a good solid sitting position, to be certain of placing a bullet in the chest cavity of deer or antelope out at 400 yards or more.

In the Canadian north I usually wear a down jacket, and many times I have rolled it up and used it on a stone or hummock for a steady rest. In Wyoming antelope hunting, I have used the same rolled-up jacket on clumps of sage. Once in a while a man can put a 10-gallon hat in the crotch of a tree and use it as a rest. The rifleman should never lay the fore-end of the rifle on anything hard, because if he does the rifle will jump up from the hard surface and his shot will be high.

Just as the finest practice for the running-game shooter is popping at galloping jackrabbits, the best possible practice for the long-range big-game shot is long-range shooting of woodchucks, prairy dogs, and coyotes, and the illusive crow.

In taking a long shot, this youth uses a ridge comb as a rest and his jacket rolled up as a pad. Such a set-up provides nearly all the advantages of a bench rest.

This little essay is not an endorsement of promiscuous long-range shooting. From a humanitarian standpoint the less of it done—even by a good shot—the better. But the time does come when circumstances are right, and then an expert rifleman can save his bacon by making a hit at long range.

First of all, the animal should be nondangerous. He should be in the open so bullet effect can be judged and the first shot followed up with others if it is not fatal. The hunter should have an accurate flat-shooting rifle, sighted in for the longest possible range which will not cause midrange misses. He should be able to judge range fairly well by mentally marking off the distances in 100-yard units or by comparing the size of an animal with a reticule of known value. He should know the drop at various ranges of the bullet he is using, and if his memory is poor he should affix the data to the buttstock of his rifle with transparent waterproof tape. He should shoot from the steadiest position he can assume, and then he should squeeze the trigger and hope for the best.

Never should he attempt a shot from an unsteady position, nor when the animal can get out of sight quickly. He should avoid shooting at long range if it seems possible to move within his sure hitting range, even if he has to come back the next day to make the stalk. When he does try long-range shooting he should use every means at his command to do the job exactly right!

I have had many letters from those who think it would be a great idea to supply themselves with some sort of a portable rangefinder so that they could look at a buck or a bull elk way out yonder and tell just how far he was away. For many reasons the idea, though seductive, is not practical. For certain uses the split-image rangefinders used on some miniature cameras is very successful. I have one in an old Zeiss Contax. It has two prisms and when the images of both prisms come together the camera is in focus and you can read the range off. If something is 3 feet or 5 feet away, the rangefinder knows exactly. It can tell the difference between 25 and 50 feet and between 50 feet and 100 feet, but to my rangefinder a house down the block 100 yards away and the moon are the same distance.

Artillery rangefinders use the same principle but the prisms are from 4 to 6 feet apart. They are too heavy and bulky to carry hunting. A portable split-image rangefinder is made. This will give you the range pretty accurately at ranges where you do not need the information. A modern high-velocity rifle like the .270 and the 7mm Remington Magnum can be sighted in for 250–300 yards. Up to 350 yards or so a hit can be obtained by holding a bit higher on the animal. If the bullet will strike a few inches from where the reticule rests to 350 yards or so, who needs a range-finder?

16

Double, Pump, or Automatic?

ONCE UPON A TIME the shooter about to invest in a new shotgun did some heavy thinking on just what type of smoothbore he would lay out his money for. Would it be a double, a pump, or an automatic? If he did his brooding prior to the turn of the century, chances were overwhelming that he would end up with a double. If he made his choice a couple of decades later, the probability would be better than 50-50 that he would select a repeater. Right now, the man picking a new weapon will take a repeater probably nine times out of ten. Actually his struggle will be to decide which type of repeater he wants—automatic, pump, or bolt-action. Many youngsters start off with single-barrel guns, and some still lay the cash on the line for doubles—either side-by-side jobs or over-and-unders—but all in all it is the repeater that sets the play.

The United States is the stronghold of the gun firing more than one shot from a single barrel, and the double is a vanishing form. In Europe, on the other hand, the side-by-side double is the great favorite. At least one automatic has been made in Germany. Two are made in Italy. The famous Browning automatic is made in Belgium, *but* from American design and largely for sale and distribution to the United States and elsewhere out of Europe. In England, where wingshooting and modern shotgun manufacture were both born, the side-by-side double is still king, and what little competition it gets is from the over-and-under. So far as I know, no repeater has ever been made in Great Britain, and a definitive British book on the shotgun is almost entirely concerned with the double.

Are the advantages all on the side of the doubles, as the British and Continentals evidently believe, or are they all on the side of the repeaters, as Americans seem to believe? Or does the double have its advantages as well as its disadvantages? Can the same thing be said for the pump and for the automatic?

I am a double-barrel man myself—yet a double man who at the present moment has in the rack a couple of automatics and a pump. I am a double-

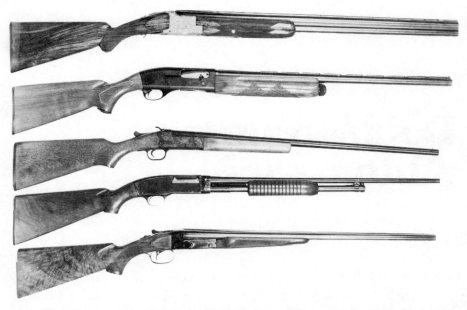

The principal types of shotguns. Top to bottom, the Browning Superposed, Remington autoloader, Harrington & Richardson single-shot, Winchester Model 42 slide-action (in .410), and Winchester Model 21 side-by-side.

barrel man who nevertheless has to admit that for whatever the reason he can break a few more skeet targets out of 100 with an automatic than he can with his favorite double.

For years the popularity of the double in the United States has been constantly declining, and fewer and fewer firms are making that form of gun. The famous Parker is no more. The Baker has long since disappeared. The Lefever is no longer made. The great old name of Ithaca appears only on pumps, and Remington has made no side-by-side doubles since 1912. The Meriden Gun Company is but a forgotten name, and so is Hopkins & Allen. Iver Johnson no longer makes doubles. The last war put the skids under the high-grade Fox guns, and the L. C. Smith guns will probably never again be made. The Savage-Stevens combination turns out a lot of inexpensive doubles. Winchester has long since discontinued the double Model 24. At the present time, the only premium-grade side-by-side double manufactured in the United States is the Winchester Model 21, a relative newcomer in the field.

What is the explanation for this rout of the side-by-side double? Is it basically inferior to the pump, the automatic, to the over-and-under? Why is it that Americans are overwhelmingly shooters of repeating shotguns, whereas Europeans are just as strong for the older type of gun?

Part of the explanation, I believe, is that double-gun manufacturers were in the past an intensely conservative lot. The standard double gun always had a little splinter fore-end that was too thin, too short. With it the gunner couldn't get his left hand out to swing his barrels fast and unless he watched himself he was apt to get his fingers singed on the hot barrels. The pump or automatic, by the very nature of its construction, had to have a fore-end a man could hang onto, and for that reason many found they could shoot better with repeaters.

Double triggers were always standard on double-barrel shotguns. Many have professed to see a great advantage in double triggers. I never have. If the length of pull is right for the front trigger, it is wrong for the rear trigger, and vice versa. If the double-gun buyer wanted a selective single trigger, it cost him from $30 to $100 extra, just as a beavertail fore-end cost him extra. Likewise, if our boy wanted automatic ejectors, he had to pay extra for them in most grades. By the time the customer had got a shotgun with the necessary "extras" on it, he had laid out enough for two or three

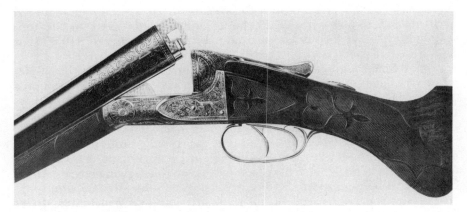

Engraving on a very expensive Holland & Holland side-by-side (above), and a high-grade Fox (below).

pumps. Long ago, the manufacturers of doubles should have worked out good inexpensive nonselective single triggers and should have made them standard. Likewise they should have made beavertail fore-ends standard, and, if possible, automatic ejectors. They should also have discontinued automatic safeties, which are, in my opinion, strictly an invention of the devil.

But probably the greatest factor in the decline of the double in the United States was the cost. Labor in the United States comes high, and the good double gun takes a lot of labor in finishing and adjusting. Some years ago, I slyly gathered some figures in the room where high-class doubles of a certain make were being assembled. The guns were at least three-fourths finished when they were received. The barrels were joined, actions and parts were finish-machined, stocks machine-inletted and turned. Guns were reamed out at the muzzle for the degree of choke ordered, parts were hand-fitted, adjusted, and tested. Butt stocks and fore-ends were fitted, finished, checkered. Metal parts were sent out to be blued. If I remember correctly, thirty-five men in the assembling room were turning out about seven finished doubles a day. They were very fine guns, but they cost important money.

All over the world the price of good double-barrel shotguns has skyrocketed. In 1940 I bought for my wife a Winchester Model 21 in skeet grade. It had no engraving but it was beautifully finished, perfectly adjusted. The stock was of well-marked American walnut and the checkering was extensive and good. If my memory serves me well I paid $115 for it. It has been used in the field and at skeet for thirty-seven years and has performed perfectly. The cheapest Winchester Model 21 now costs about $3,000.

I once bought in Rome a lovely little 20-gauge Beretta over-and-under, the AS EELL model. I paid $660 plus duty for it. It weighed a bit less than 6 pounds and was so light I never shot it very well. I sold it for $2,000. This model now brings over $3,000 secondhand in Italy! As I write this in the winter of 1977 my pet of pets is a 12-gauge Beretta side-by-side sidelock known as the Model 450 EL. Along around the middle 1960s I paid something over $1,000 for the gun with two sets of barrels (28-inch modified and full and 26-inch improved cylinder and modified) and an oak-and-leather trunk case with brass hardware. I have been offered $10,000 for it.

A good Spanish gun that could have been purchased in Madrid for $300 a few years ago now costs over $900. Belgian prices have gone up in proportion. The Browning Superposed made in Belgium is now indeed a luxury item. A British Holland and Holland or Purdey that cost $3,000 in the early 1960s now costs at least three times as much.

Bill Ruger, president of Sturm, Ruger, has recently brought out a handsome over-and-under 20-gauge with single triggers and automatic ejectors at around $500 in 1978. He has a side-by-side on the drawing boards. Many doubles are being imported, some from Japan, some from Spain, some from Italy. Some are excellent but some are not. The Winchester Model 101 over-and-under guns are made in Japan under Winchester supervision. I have the "skeet set," with 20-gauge, 28-gauge, and .410 barrels. I like it very much. The good Japanese SKB guns formerly imported by

The Winchester Model 101 over-under is made in Japan for Winchester.

Ithaca and marketed as the Ithaca-SKB are now being distributed by a subsidiary of the Japanese manufacturer. The Weatherby double over-and-unders are made in Italy.

Handwork is the bane of the fine double. In order to work satisfactorily, the good double must be made to small tolerances. The selective single trigger is a gadget as delicate and complicated as a watch. So are selective automatic ejectors.

It is easy to sit down and list the disadvantages of the double. It is expensive and it is complicated. If a man who owns one wants to vary his choke, he has to get an extra pair of expensive barrels, whereas if he has a pump or automatic, he simply can get a variable-choke device put on.

Nevertheless, the fine double is to many the greatest scattergun in the world. With good barrel length it can still be short overall. Because it does not have a long receiver like the pump or automatic, the weight is more between the hands, and it is a sweet, lively thing to swing and shoot. To the confirmed double fancier no gun made can compete with a good double in balance and handling qualities. Nor can any other type of shotgun compete with it in looks.

The double is in many ways the safest of all shotguns. When one opens the action he can tell at a glance if it is loaded or not. It is also quick and easy to see if there is an obstruction in the barrel—and obstructions are *the* reason for burst barrels. If a gunner wants to cross a fence, all he has to do is to break his gun and even if there are shells in the chambers it is absolutely impossible for it to fire. The tang safety on the double gun is in the natural place, where a flick of the thumb will put the safety off or on. It is much faster and more convenient than the trigger-guard safeties on pumps and automatics.

Quick choke selectivity is also a great advantage the double has over any other type of gun. The upland hunter who takes his first bird at 25 yards and his second at 35 has precisely the right boring in improved cylinder and modified. The duck hunter can use his full-choke barrel for pass shooting, his modified barrel for the first shot on decoyed ducks. For balance, handling qualities, and safety, the double is in a class by itself.

The over-and-under has in recent years been gaining in popularity as the side-by-side double has been losing it. Most famous in this country of the over-and-unders is the Browning Superposed manufactured in Belgium to the design of the late John Browning and sold in this country by the Browning Arms Co. Anything that has been said about the side-by-side double can be said about the over-and-under. It is complicated, expensive to manufacture; but it is also a lively, fast-pointing, well-balanced gun with

A pre-1962 Winchester Model 12 pump-action.

the further advantage of the single sighting plane that one gets with the pump or automatic. Marlin once made a handsome over-and-under at about half the price of the beautiful Brownings but without single trigger and automatic ejectors. Other beauties are made in England, Germany, Austria, and Spain at prices which compete with the Browning and also at prices that are about like those asked for a four-door sedan f.o.b. Detroit. The British guns particularly can run into money. Pal of mine had a matched pair of 12-gauge over-and-unders. For the price he paid for them he could have bought a couple of Cadillacs.

Probably the most durable gun ever to be made is the American pump, which began to take over an enormous share of the shotgun market when the Winchester Model 97, which was dropped in 1964, was developed from the old Winchester Model 93. The Model 97 was the first genuinely successful pump, although there had been earlier guns of the type, the Spencer and the Burgess. It immediately started cutting into the double-gun sales, and it pushed the Winchester lever-action shotguns into oblivion. The hammer Model 97 was followed by the hammerless Model 12 Winchester, by the Remington pumps which have culminated in the current Model 870, by the Savage and Stevens pumps, by the Ithaca, Marlins, and lately the Nobel.

The pump is always a good bet. Many like the single sighting plane. Many also believe that the fact that it is manually operated makes it more deadly since the man behind it settles down for his next shot as he works the slide. The pump is rugged, relatively cheap, and easy to repair. The man who wants to use one as an all-around gun can get a spare barrel of different length or choke for no great amount of sugar or he can simply have one of the variable-choke devices put on. The pump is, alas, a sort of a rattly gadget, and there are those who claim there was never such a thing as a good-looking pump gun. But tastes vary in guns as they do in horses.

In the days when big limits on wildfowl were allowed and before magazine capacity was limited, the pump in the hands of an expert was probably the deadliest duck gun ever designed. I once saw an old-timer who had been a market hunter in his day cut down five ducks from a flock, and a good many times I have seen fast men with pumps make triples on quail and Huns, as well as on ducks.

Pumps are available in every style from the plainest to the fanciest, with plain barrels, matted ribs, ventilated ribs. They are favorites at trap shooting and at skeet, in the duck blinds and in the uplands. Pumps have been made in .410, 28, 16, 12, and 12 gauge Magnum—and millions have been sold. So popular has the pump been that it is safe to say that the typical American shotgun is a pump with a 28-inch barrel in 12 gauge.

Just as the pump has for more than a half-century been cutting into the

The boxy Browning autoloader is a favorite.

sales of double guns, the automatic has been competing with the pump. Someday the automatic may become the No. 1 American shotgun. At one time the automatic was, in 12 gauge, always heavy, often clumsy, slow to handle. Usually the lines were also homely. At one time the user of the automatic was looked down upon in conservative quarters as being a congenial low-life and probably a game hog.

The automatic is little, if any, more expensive to manufacture than the pump, and it has some very great advantages over the pump. For one thing it has built-in automatic ejection. It is the most foolproof of all shotguns. It is easy for the excited shooter of a pump to balk it and make it malfunction. With the automatic, though, all the man shooting it has to do is to pull the trigger. The automatic of suitable weight, gauge, and choke is a poisonous upland gun, a crack duck gun, and the favorite among skeet guns. Like the pump it lends itself to being equipped either with a variable-choke device or with a barrel of another boring at no great expense. An enormous advantage is that the operating of the repeating mechanism absorbs around 30 percent of the recoil, a factor which is exceedingly important in skeet shooting and also important in the duck blind. It is my opinion that as the years go by, the automatic is going to make it tougher and tougher for the pump.

In recent years, many bolt-action shotguns have been turned out. Their primary advantage is that because they are cheap to manufacture, they open up a market where every dollar counts. They are boys' guns, utility farm guns to leave in the corner of the barn to use in case a chicken hawk comes prowling around, meat guns to be taken along to pot grouse and ptarmigan with on a rough wilderness trip. They are sound guns and many of them handle and point very well. Their great disadvantage is that they are so slow for the second shot that it is almost impossible to make a double (much less a triple) with them. The bolt action has no virtues in itself except the strength that is necessary in a high-powered rifle using cartridges that give pressures running around 50,000 pounds per square inch. Compared with the double and its single trigger, the automatic, or even the pump, the bolt-action is miserably slow.

A lever-action shotgun is faster than the bolt, but still a long way behind the other types in speed. Winchester made the Model 1887 lever-action in 12 and 10 gauge from 1887 to 1901 and the Model 1901, which was a strengthened and redesigned Model 1887, in 10 gauge only, until 1920.

Cheapest of all shotguns and one of the most widely used is the single-barrel. Many of them handle and balance beautifully, and if the user does not want to get off a fast second shot, he can do just as well with a single barrel as with anything. The single is a good safe gun for a youngster to learn to hunt with, and possibly the knowledge that he has but one shot may make him a more careful hunter than if he had a whole magazine.

The shotgun buyer probably gets the most for his money with a pump or automatic, and if he doesn't have to watch the nickels too hard the most ultimate gun satisfaction with a high-grade double, either side-by-side or over-and-under. But he can kill anything a shotgun is used on just as dead, shoot just as tight patterns, with a beat-up old single-barrel, just as it is possible for some freckled kid to catch just as big a trout with a willow pole as the skilled angler can with a $300 handmade job of split bamboo. Single trigger, automatic ejectors, engraving, and fancy checking don't make a gun shoot one bit harder, nor do they help it hit unless it is pointed right.

17

The Choice of Shotgun Gauges

AT THIS LATE DATE it is no classified secret that shotgun gauges get their names from the number of round balls of pure lead and of bore diameter that will make up a pound. There are ten 10-gauge balls in a pound, twelve balls in 12 gauge, sixteen balls in 16 gauge, and so on. The one exception is the so-called .410 "gauge," which isn't a gauge at all but a caliber and named like any rifle caliber in thousandths of an inch. The gauge system began, I believe, in England, but it is used wherever shotguns are manufactured, be it England, Spain, Belgium, or anywhere else. The British, however, usually refer to "12 bore" gune rather than "12-gauge" guns, and some continental guns are marked "Cal. 12."

The world's rifle cartridges differ enormously. Each country has its favorites. The very popular German 7 x 64 cartridge has never been loaded in the United States, for example, and the popular American .270 was never loaded in Germany. Likewise the British have loaded only a few widely used American cartridges, and in this country we have never even heard of dozens of excellently designed British centerfire metallics.

But with shotguns, it is different. A 12-gauge bore is a 12-gauge bore all over the world. Likewise a 16 and a 20 gauge, and if chamber length is all right, American shotshells can be used in foreign guns and foreign ammunition in American guns.

A switcheroo is that the nomenclature originated before the days of choke boring, and now a 12-gauge ball of bore diameter is *not* used in a 12-gauge gun because, although it would be of correct size for the *bore*, it would be too small for the muzzle, where the choke is, by anywhere from 40/1000 inch in the case of a gun with extreme full choke to 10/1000 inch in case of a gun bored to give strong improved cylinder or "quarter choke" patterns. Consequently shotgun ball cartridges in 12 gauge are loaded not with 12-gauge balls but with balls that would run about fourteen to the pound, and 16-gauge ball cartridges are loaded with balls that run around eighteen to the pound.

109

Federal shotshells in 16, 20, and 12 gauge. Below the 12-gauge shell is the powder, and to the right is the shot in the plastic shot protector and the primer.

In muzzle-loading days, guns were built in 4 gauge and 6 gauge, but I have never seen a breechloader larger than 8 gauge. In early breech-loading days, the 10-gauge gun was standard size and the man who used a 12-gauge was a small-bore addict and thought of as a daring and reckless fellow. The real wildfowl gun was the 8-gauge. When I was a kid an uncle of mine had a cherished 8-gauge Greener with hammers and Damascus barrels and I was dying to shoot it. I finally sneaked it out and salivated a couple of mallards on a pothole with it. That ponderous cannon kicked me back 3 feet and sent up a cloud of gray smoke so dense that it was some seconds before I could see the cadavers of my two puddle ducks floating on the water.

Several factors conspired to put the skids under the 8-gauge. For one thing, 8-gauge guns were very heavy and clumsy clubs that were difficult to carry, swing, and shoot. In the second place choke boring and better ammunition made their great charge of shot unnecessary to obtain sufficient pattern density for long-range kills. Final blow was struck when the big

Actual bore sizes of the six gauges most commonly used in the United States.

guns were outlawed by the federal government for use on migratory birds, just prior to World War I. Ammunition has not been manufactured for years in this country, and an 8-gauge gun or even an 8-gauge shell now is a curiosity.

The fate of the 8-gauge has pretty much overtaken the 10. Through the 1880s and 1890s the 12-gauge began to displace the 10-gauge for upland shooting because it was lighter, handier, and for the most part just as effective. As interest in the 10-gauge waned, the loading companies paid less attention to the ammunition until for years the only 10-gauge shells obtainable were loaded with $1^1/_4$ ounces of shot, the same amount to be had in ordinary high-base 12-gauge shells. The curious old Winchester lever-action repeating shotguns in Model 1901 were made in 10 gauge, but the more popular and handier Model 1897 and Model 1912 guns were not something which helped to contribute to the downfall of the 10.

Prior to World War II there was some slight survival of interest in the 10-gauge. High-speed loads with $1^5/_8$ ounces of shot in standard $2^7/_8$-inch cases became available and stepped up the power of the 10. However, the loads were unsafe in many of the older guns, particularly those with twist or Damascus barrels. Furthermore the same amount of shot was available in the 3-inch 12-gauge Magnum shell, which came along at about the same time. Along in the 1930s, Western Cartridge Co. pioneered the $3^1/_2$-inch 10-gauge Magnum shell (which was really, as far as shot charge went, an 8-gauge making like a 10) and both Ithaca and Parker built 10-gauge Magnum doubles. This Roman candle used 2 ounces of big shot at high velocity, and the man husky and astute enough to swing and point one of those ponderous doubles could make kills at astonishing ranges, often knocking a duck out of a flock at 100 yards, or picking off a single at 75 or 80.

But, alas, the demand for those Super 10s was small. The fine old Parkers just ain't no more, in 10 or any other gauge; and Ithaca, sad to say, has heeded the siren's call of the pump, which is much easier to manufacture, and no longer makes any sort of a double. Ammunition in 10-gauge Magnum is still loaded in small quantities, but at the present time the man who wants a 10-gauge double obtains it from abroad. Single- and double-barrel shotguns in 10 gauge Magnum have been imported from Spain. Ithaca has made an automatic for the big shell.

In reality, the 10-gauge is on the skids now, just as the 8-gauge was in the early part of the century. Less than 1 percent of shotshells sold annually by the big loading companies are 10-gauge. The handwriting is on the wall!

The gun that has really done all the larger ones to death is the 12-gauge, the standard gauge all over the world. The 12 is the world's standard for skeet and trap shooting, the world's favorite waterfowl gun, the world's favorite all-purpose gun, and surely in the United States it is the gun most used in upland hunting. Shells for the 12-gauge Magnum are 3 inches long and are loaded like a 10-gauge. The standard upland load with its $2^3/_4$-inch case and $1^1/_8$ ounces of shot is loaded like a 16. In England the standard 12-gauge upland load has a $2^1/_2$-inch case and $1^1/_{16}$ ounces of shot, and 12-gauge guns are even made to take 2-inch shells loaded with 1 ounce of shot—a 20-gauge load.

More and more the 12-gauge steps on the toes of the other gauges. Time

was when almost all 12-bore doubles made in this country had 30-inch barrels and weighed 8–8$^1/_2$ pounds. Most 12-gauge pumps and autos were
likewise heavy and clumsy. Such cannons were not upland guns and a man
using one of them was handicapping himself almost as much as if he had
gone afield with a ball and chain around his leg or carrying a midget on his
back.

Now the new pumps and automatics in 12-gauge are as light as 16s and
20s used to be, and the 12-gauge has further encroached on the field of the
other gauges. Lightest 12-gauge load available today for upland shooting is
the trap load with 1$^1/_8$ ounces of No. 7$^1/_2$ or No. 8 shot with 2$^3/_4$–3 drams
of powder, which are actually just about 16-gauge loads and have about the
same recoil and report. With the new 12s weighing like 16s and 20s and
with recoil-reducing gimmicks *kicking* like 20s, I wonder what the outcome
is going to be!

In England the 12 is even more the universal gauge than it is in the United States, and the famous London gunmakers there turn out 12s as light as
6 pounds with barrels as short as 25 inches. No American 12-gauge doubles
that light have ever been made, because the American 12 tends to be an all-
around gun and even the very lightest American 12-gauge load has always
been a fairly husky one by British standards. Americans have been experi-
menting with Magnum 12s now for twenty years or more. Fox, Parker, and
Smith used to make heavy 12s chambered for 3-inch shells and 1$^3/_8$–1$^5/_8$
ounces of shot; but the Magnums never became very popular until Winchester brought out the Model 12 Heavy Duck Gun for the 3-inch Magnum,
practically a 10 wearing a 12-gauge sign.

For many years the 16-gauge was next in popularity to the 12-gauge.
However, since the end of World War II the 16 has fallen out of favor.
There are many reasons for this. One is that the 16-gauge is little used in
trap or skeet since it has to compete against the 12 in the "all-gauge" class.
Most trap clubs do not even stock 16-gauge shells. For another thing, the
advent of the 20-gauge Magnum with the 3-inch shell has hurt the 16.
There is nothing that the 16 can do that the 20-gauge cannot do as well or
perhaps better. The 16-gauge in the last couple of generations has never
been loaded in 3-inch cases. In the 16-gauge 2$^3/_4$-inch Magnum the load is
1$^1/_4$ ounces of shot, the same as in the 3-inch 20-gauge.

At one time the 16-gauge was very popular in Europe, particularly in
Germany, France, and Belgium. England, Spain, and Italy remained
12-gauge country. In Germany many thousands of three-barrel guns
("drillings") were made with two 16-gauge barrels over a rifle barrel that
was often for the 8 x 57JR cartridge. Now, I am told, the 16 is in a crash
decline on the European continent. In the United States some of the
repeating shotguns are not made in 16 gauge at all. In Idaho where I live,
16-gauge shotshells are often difficult to come by. Be that as it may, a
16-gauge double of good quality is handsome and fast-handling. Good
used ones can usually be obtained cheaper than 12s or 20s.

In the 20-gauge we are coming to another sort of gun, the lightest, trim-
mest of all guns that can be considered real catch-as-catch-can hunting
guns. For the chap who has to walk long distances and lug a gun over hill
and dale in upland hunting, the 20 is it. There is no handsomer, racier-

looking gun than a sleek 20-gauge double with 26-inch barrels and all classed up with beavertail fore-end, ejectors, and single trigger. The little pumps in that gauge are also very sweet to handle. Just as the 12 has more range than the 16, the 16 has more range than the 20; but the lighter gun gets on the target faster and thus the handicap is more apparent than real.

Furthermore, a full-choked 20-gauge has about all the range most of us can handle, even on waterfowl. With 1 ounce of No. 6 (about the largest shot that should be used) a good-patterning 20-gauge will take single ducks to a good 45 yards—and not many gunners can hit them farther away than that with anything. During the early part of the depression things were tough with the O'Connors and I was hard put to keep my wife and young in hog jowl and hoecakes. The family scattergun arsenal was down to two 20-gauge doubles, an L. C. Smith and an Ithaca. It was very seldom that we missed a bird that we would have hit with a 12-gauge. Once the 20 was loaded with only $^3/_4$ ounce of shot. Now the "standard" load is $^7/_8$ ounce and the maximum load of the Super-X, Nitro Express variety is 1 ounce.

Possibly 18- and 14-gauge breech-loading shotguns have been made in the United States, though I have never seen one. They have been made in Europe, though, as every now and then a correspondent writes in for identification of a gun so marked. Muzzleloaders in those gauges were quite common.

The 28-gauge has never been very popular. Parker used to make 28-gauge doubles, and I believe Ithaca also did. Winchester made a 28-gauge in the Model 12 pump gun and Remington in the Model 11-48 automatic. Both are largely used in small-bore skeet shooting. The modern 28-gauge shell is loaded with $^3/_4$ ounce of shot, what the old 20-gauge load used to be. Because the shot column is shorter and pressure lower, the 28 patterns somewhat better than the .410 and has the edge in skeet competition. Chambers of 28-gauge guns were changed from $2^1/_2$ to $2^3/_4$ inches in the early 1930s. Twenty-eight-gauge "magnum" shells have been loaded with $^7/_8$ and 1 ounce of shot.

Let no one think that the 28 is a toy. A man with whom I hunt now and then has a Parker DHE grade 28 with 26-inch barrels, and I have seen him knock down cock pheasants at very respectable ranges. Like 20-gauge ammunition, 28-gauge stuff is light and easy to lug around, a great advantage that the small-bores have over the ponderous 12s.

Our 28 is a nice little gun, particularly for the young shooter who is recoil-sensitive, but ammunition is so poorly distributed that in many areas obtaining it takes a good deal of staff work. It is too much like a 20 ever to be very popular.

The .410 "gauge" is more popular than the 28, and at one time or another a vast number of guns have been made for it, from little pot-metal single-barrels that sold for five bucks or so through the sleek and handsome little Winchester Model 42 to the flossiest Parker and Ithaca doubles.

Not too many years ago the .410 was made with $2^1/_2$-inch chambers, and the most shot one could get in one of the diminutive shells was $^3/_8$ ounce. Then Winchester brought out the Model 42 pump and the 3-inch .410 shell using $^3/_4$ ounce of shot, a move which definitely took the .410 out of the popgun class.

The old .410 shells were loaded with $^3/_8$ ounce of shot and even with a full-choke gun patterns were so thin that kills were very difficult to make at over 25 yards. Once when I was a lad, I borrowed a nice-looking little double .410 from a friend and tried to shoot squirrels with it. The experiment was not successful because the squirrel is a tough little beast and I couldn't get enough shot on one.

Today the .410 is loaded in $2^1/_2$-inch cases with $^1/_2$ ounce of shot and in 3-inch cases with $^3/_4$ ounce. Only use for the $^1/_2$-ounce load is sub-small-bore skeet shooting, but the $^3/_4$-ounce load is a practical game load with No. $7^1/_2$ and No. 9 shot to 30 yards.

There are many myths connected with shotguns, and one of the principal ones is that the smaller the gauge, the smaller the pattern. It ain't so. Exactly the same standards govern 12, 16, and 20 and a full-choke gun of any gauge is one that will put 70 percent of the shot charge into a 30-inch circle at 40 yards. Only the standard for the .410 is different. A full-choke .410 is one that will put 70 percent of its pattern into a 24-inch circle at 25 yards.

The smaller gauges, then, do not shoot smaller patterns, given the same type of choke. They simply shoot thinner patterns. If the same amount of shot is used, the smaller the gauge the more difficult it is to obtain dense patterns, since the shot column is longer and there is more shot deformation. Actually, there must be a terrific amount of shot deformation in the very long column of the .410 with $^3/_4$ ounce of shot, since beyond 30–35 yards a .410 pattern simply disintegrates. Just try patterning a .410 at 40 yards sometime?

A 12-gauge will handle $1^1/_8$ ounces of shot better than a 16, and 1 ounce of shot better than a 20. The smaller the gauge, the higher the pressures, as a rule, and because the pressures are higher, the percentage of deformed and useless shot pellets is also higher.

Since patterns run thinner in the smaller gauges, they are less effective with larger shot. Whereas a full-choked 12 will maintain sufficient pattern density with No. 4s to kill a mallard, let us say, at 50 yards, one should probably drop to No. 5 in a 16, and to No. 6 in a 20-gauge. With a .410 or a 28-gauge, patterns with anything larger than No. $7^1/_2$ aren't too hot, and I have had more luck on upland game with No. 9 skeet loads in a .410 than with any other shot size.

As to the popularity of the various gauges, one outfit, which does not make a .410, in a recent fiscal year sold 52 percent 12-gauge guns, 30 percent 16-gauge guns, and 17 percent 20s. My own hunch is that now that the light 12-gauge repeater is with us, figures will swing even more in favor of the larger gauge.

18

The Shotgun Stock

TO BE SATISFACTORY the shotgun stock should be properly designed, and it should fit the man who is to use it. Ideally, it should also be a thing of grace and beauty.

The best-designed and handsomest stock in the world is of no use as a practical shooting weapon if it does not fit.

In the past twenty years volumes have been written on the design of rifle stocks. Hundreds of custom makers have sprung up to give the boys the sort of rifles they want, presumably fitting the owners like well-worn shoes. On the other hand, very little has been written about shotgun stocks, and a custom stocker who depends on shotgun work alone would soon be starving.

This is very curious circumstance indeed, because the nature of shotgun shooting makes correct design and exact fit more important than in rifle shooting. The crack rifle shot can, if he has to, do good shooting with almost any sort of stock, as shown by the fine scores made with the miserably designed and proportioned stock on the old 1903 Springfield.

The reason the shotgun stock is relatively so much more important than the rifle stock is that the man who shoots the scattergun has so little time to work with. Even on running game, the rifleman usually very often has four or five seconds to play with. On standing game he has relatively all the time in the world. Compared to the speed necessary in shotgun shooting, even the target rifleman shooting a rapid-fire course has time to burn.

The skeet or trap shot takes about one second to break his target if he is fast, one and a half seconds if he is slow. If he takes two seconds he is as slow as the seven-year itch. The good skeet shot shooting doubles breaks both targets in the doubles in one and a half seconds, and the really fast characters break them in a second. The boys who do some clay target shooting in the off season to keep their reactions functioning and the eyes

115

When checking stockgun fit, press your cheek hard against the stock. If it's right, you'll look straight down the barrel. In actual shooting, though, cheek the stock firmly but not hard. Then your eye will see the barrel foreshortened a bit and you'll shoot up.

focused are generally the best and fastest game shots, as speed is as necessary in the hunting field as it is at the skeet or trap layout. When a cock pheasant gets up at 35 yards it takes a fast shot to kill him clean while he is still in range instead of feathering and crippling him.

Good design and correct fit of the gunstock is an enormously important factor in speed. If the gun comes up pointed right and instantly on, shooting fast comes naturally. If, on the other hand, the gunner has to jockey his musket around to line it up (or aim it) he cannot help being a slow, dawdling shot. The rifleman can fit himself to his stock, but the shotgun shooter should be fitted by his stock.

To me the acid test of gun fit is to shoot a round of skeet. Then if there is anything sour about the gun fit, it is quickly apparent. If the stock is a bit too long, the comb too high, the pitch wrong, it doesn't take long to find out.

The classic shotgun stock originated in England well over one hundred years ago, and the great old muzzle-loading, flintlock doubles turned out by such masters as Joseph Manton, with their straight grips, wide butts, and moderate drop at comb and heel still handle well and are still things of beauty. British, Belgian, and French shotguns still pretty much follow this pattern. The straight grip is almost universal because Europeans have never gone in for pumps and automatics and they have seldom used single triggers on their doubles. Fore-ends have clean lines but have remained skimpy little splinters that are hard to hold and which do not do much of a job of keeping the hand away from the hot barrels.

The Americans and the Germans were both primarily nations of rifle shooters, and in both countries the gunmakers simply tended to put rifle stocks on shotguns and let it go at that. The old-time American double gun often had a 2-inch drop at comb and a 3$^1/_2$-inch drop at heel, and most German shotguns had pistol grips, even though they had double triggers —again showing the rifle influence. This excessive drop at both comb and

heel tended to make both Americans and Germans aimers instead of point-
ers, and because they were aimers they tended to be slow and pokey shots.
With a gun so stocked one can shoot only by consciously lining up the rib or
the two sights—aiming, in other words. This rifle-mindedness is also shown
by the fact that both Germans and Americans thought of the shotgun as a
long-range weapon, and after choke boring came along, most guns were
bored full and full or modified and full, whereas the British guns tended to
be much more open.

Most changes in stock design have come not from the influence of field
shooters but from that of trap and skeet shooters. The field shot doesn't
have anyone to keep score on him. He can miss four birds out of five. He
can pot a covey on the ground or a bunny on the sit and for bragging purposes his bag is just as good as if he averaged 50 percent or better on the
run. Shooting at clay birds, though, is done before witnesses and unkind
people keep score.

When Americans began trap shooting, they soon discovered that the
guns they had been using on game were not so good. Because of their
crooked stocks, they were slow to get on with, and because they were used
to aiming right down the rib, they tended to undershoot their targets. The
boys also found that with their crooked stocks their elevation tended to be
sour because every time they placed their cheeks a bit differently on the
sloping comb they were changing their sighting. The little splinter
fore-ends on the conventional doubles kept them from taking up recoil with
the left hand, and firing seventy-five to a hundred 12-gauge trap loads a
day beat them to death.

Trap shooting was responsible for the development in the United States
of the straighter buttstock, which cut down on recoil since the kick came
back in a straight line. It resulted in high-comb stocks which made the pattern go high to intercept the rapidly rising clay target. The Monte Carlo
comb became popular on the trap gun, as this type of comb gives uniform
elevation. The beavertail fore-end was developed because with it the left
hand is farther out. This enables the shooter to swing and control his piece
better and also to take up recoil with his left hand.

Some of these developments were useful for the field gun. The beavertail fore-end on the double and the big, hand-filling "trap" fore-end on the
pump or automatic is very useful in the field. The straight-stocked trap gun
also influenced the design of field guns, and the use of the single trigger on
doubles and on pumps and automatics caused the design of better pistol
grips on doubles.

Skeet began as a game by which upland gunners could do some off-
season practice, and the first skeet guns were simply ordinary upland guns,
mostly bored improved cylinder and modified but some bored full and
modified. Barrels were 28 inches as a rule and sometimes even 30 inches.

Before long, though, the lads were getting pattern-conscious and stock-
conscious. Barrels were chopped off and opened up. Beavertail fore-ends
began to blossom out. As a skeet gun for competition shooting the side-
by-side double is pretty much out of the running. However, the Winchester Model 21, which I consider the finest-stocked double in the world, is
pretty largely a product of the lessons in design learned on the skeet field.

A well-designed shotgun stock should have a hand-filling fore-end for speed and sureness in pointing and for taking up recoil, and the fore-end should extend far enough forward so that the left hand will have plenty of leverage. The buttstock itself should be relatively straight, with never more than 1 inch greater drop at heel than at comb, because the crooked stock causes the comb to bang up against the cheek and accentuate recoil and also because the crooked stock is slower to point, just as a carpenter's square is slower to point than a ruler. The man with very square shoulders can take a drop at heel only $\frac{1}{2}$ inch greater than drop at comb. About $\frac{3}{4}$ inch greater drop at heel seems right for me, and few people need more than 1 inch.

The comb should be rounded and thick enough to put the eye right in line with the rib. A comb that is too thick or too thin will make a gun crossfire, and a too-thick comb bruises the cheek if the gunner crowds down to line up with the rib.

I like the sleek handsome lines of the gun with the straight grip, but in these days of repeating shotguns and doubles with single triggers there is little excuse for the straight grip in spite of its racy looks. The grip should

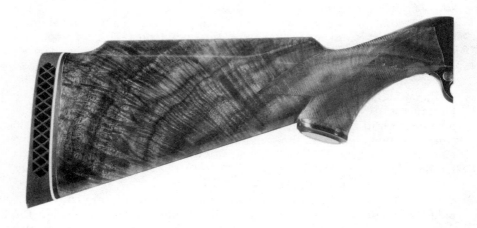

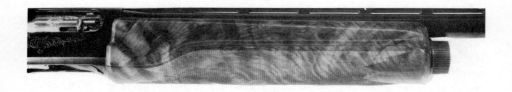

The buttstock and fore-end of an autoloader. This one is of very high-quality figured American walnut. In the author's opinion a fore-end should be big and hand-filling.

support the hand naturally without cramping. The best grip is not the old half pistol grip of the shotgun or the full pistol grip of the rifle but a compromise. Straight grips cramp the wrist and tend to make the piece shoot high. Too-full grips are slow in the field.

The Monte Carlo comb, although useful on the trap gun, is no thing of beauty, and it is not necessary on the gun with little drop at heel since the stock is straight enough to maintain elevation anyway. Putting a cheekpiece on a shotgun stock shows that whoever orders such a stock is thinking in the terms of rifle shooting. With more time the rifle shot can cheek his piece very firmly. The shotgun shot does not. Not long ago I read a piece by a chap who had got a shotgun and a rifle stocked with identical stocks. It does not take a very astute person to dope out that our boy didn't know much about shooting a shotgun.

Design of factory shotgun stocks has improved vastly in the past forty years. Nowadays the stock on the Winchester Model 21 double is perfection. Those on the Remington Model 1100 automatic and the Model 870 Remington pump are excellent. Another fine stock is that on the Winchester Model 12 skeet and trap gun and on the late Model 42 Winchester .410 pump, which, by the way, is exactly to the same dimensions as the stock on my Model 21 Winchester double.

How should a stock fit?

For skeet shooting and for all-around hunting, the comb should be high enough so that if the cheek is pressed *hard* against the comb, the eye will look right down the barrel. If by pressing the cheek hard, the eye is below the barrel and only the receiver can be seen, the comb has too much drop. The gun will tend to shoot low and if the barrel is seen properly, the cheek will not be against the comb at all, and the shooter will tend to be an arm swinger instead of a body swinger. If, on the other hand, the whole barrel is seen foreshortened when the cheek is pressed hard against the comb, the gun will shoot high. For skeet shooting and for general hunting, a high-shooting gun like this is poison as the charge will pass above too many targets. For trap shooting, where all shots are taken at rapidly rising targets, the high-shooting gun is correct because then the shooter can hold the muzzle on his bird yet break it. The British driven-game gun has even a higher comb and a straighter stock than the American trap gun because in this sport all the birds are overhead incomers and the high-shooting gun has a built-in lead.

The comb height and shape are the most important dimensions of the shotgun stock, because the comb is the shotgun's rear sight, controlling both elevation and windage. The too-high comb will cause overshooting, the too-low comb undershooting. The too-thick comb will cause the gun to crossfire to the left, the too-thin comb to the right. If the comb height is correct, the man behind it can simply put the muzzle on what he wants to hit and touch off. He becomes a pointer and a fast shot. If it isn't, he tends to become an aimer and a slow shot.

In field shooting or skeet shooting no one cheeks the stock hard as he does when the gun is at rest and he is holding on a mark as with a rifle. Instead, he cheeks his gun firmly, sees the barrel slightly foreshortened, and shoots at his bird a bit *up*. The shotgun is controlled by seeing the end of the barrel in relation to the target, *not* by using the receiver as a rear sight or by using the second bead on the barrel. The comb of the shotgun, then, performs the functions of the rear sight and the end of the barrel serves as the front sight. The front bead sight on a correctly stocked shotgun is ornamental but hardly useful and the second bead or rear sight is a trap to make aimers out of the unwary.

The less the drop at heel the less recoil effect is felt and the faster the gun handles. Everyone should shoot the straightest stock that mounts naturally and feels good.

The stock should be long enough to keep the right thumb away from the nose and short enough so that the gun can be mounted fast. If a stock is a bit too short the thumb will bang into the nose with recoil, particularly when an overhead shot is taken. If it is too long, the butt will catch on the clothes, slow up the mounting of the gun, and destroy the timing. A short man under 5 feet, 8 inches will be pretty well fitted with a length of pull of $13^3/_4$ inches, a man of average height with a 14-inch pull, a 6-footer with $14^1/_4$, and an exceedingly tall man with long arms with a stock $14^1/_2$ or even $14^3/_4$ inches long. These dimensions are for skeet and field shooting. Since the trap shot mounts his gun before he calls for his bird, he can use a longer stock. Since the duck shot is usually bundled up in heavy clothes, he can get a shorter stock. Any shooter can adapt himself to some extent to his stock by holding his left hand farther out on the fore-end if the stock is on the short side or farther back if the stock is too long.

The pitch of the stock is simply the angle at which the butt is cut or the plate or recoil pad set on. It is measured from the barrel. Zero pitch or pitch up tend to make the butt slip up and the shot fly low. To some extent changing pitch by putting shims under the heel or toe of the buttplate will tend to raise or lower the pattern. The sole purpose of pitch is to keep the butt comfortably on the shoulder and to keep the barrel in proper alignment.

The rubber recoil pad is a pious idea on any gun of heavy recoil, but I don't care for one on a gun to be used at skeet or in the uplands since often the rubber slows down the speed of mounting as it catches on the clothes. My favorite is the butt of plain wood checkered, or the skeleton buttplate seen on high-grade Parkers and on some fancy European guns. For that matter there is nothing wrong with the ordinary composition buttplate except its plebeian looks.

Good fit and good design of the stock are of such enormous importance to the shotgun shooter that it would be hard to exaggerate them. Anyone who aspires to be a good shot should study his gun, his shooting form, and his reactions to determine exactly what he needs until he arrives at dimensions so perfect that he can point his gun as naturally as he points a finger. No matter how good a shot a man is he will lose birds if the comb of his gun is $^1/_8$ inch too high or too low, if the pitch is an inch off, the comb too thin or too thick.

Many years ago I was shooting quail with a 20-gauge double that had too much drop but nevertheless fitted me fairly well. I traded it in on a much more expensive double with a drop at comb of $1^3/_8$, drop at heel of $1^7/_8$, and a straight grip. With the old gun I had probably been averaging around 50 percent. With the new gun my average dropped to 25 percent. I had the stock bent and my average went up again.

Various concern have try-guns with stocks which can be adjusted to give various drops, lengths of pull, and so on. The idea is for a customer to be fitted by the try-gun and then the measurements duplicated. An expert tells him when he is fitted. That sounds very nice, but it strikes me that this is a bit like laying out a set of specifications and then ordering a wife by mail through a matrimonial adviser. There is only one guy who can tell if a stock fits you and that is you—and you cannot tell until you have shot the gun and studied it.

The various standard factory guns differ in small ways in stock dimensions, and by trying the various makes in salesrooms, most gunners can find a pretty good fit. Length of pull and pitch can be easily changed, and drop at comb and heel can be changed at the factory or by bending by the hot oil process—something which can be done by either Frank Pachmayr of Los Angeles or by Griffin & Howe of New York.

But remember these points:

When your cheek is pressed hard against the comb does your eye look straight down the barrel? If so, drop at comb is right.

Does the gun come smoothly and easily to your shoulder and stay there naturally and at the same time keep your right thumb away from your nose? If so length of pull and pitch are OK.

Does your right hand feel easy and natural at the pistol grip? If it does, the design and curve are correct.

If the gun purchaser can say yes to all these questions and if in addition the gun feels good, then chances are he has a pretty good fit. If possible, though, he should take the gun out and shoot it, either at skeet or at birds thrown from a hand trap. Then if things aren't exactly right he can quickly tell it. After all, the acid test of gun stock fit and design lies in the shooting!

SOME DIMENSIONS OF STANDARD SHOTGUN STOCKS

	DROP at COMB	DROP at HEEL	LENGTH of PULL
Remington Model 11-48	$1^5/_8$	$2^1/_2$	14
Winchester Model 12, field	$1^1/_2$	$2^1/_2$	14
Winchester Model 12, trap	$1^3/_8$	$1^5/_8$	$14^1/_2$
Winchester Model 12, Monte Carlo	$1^1/_2$—$1^1/_2$		$14^2/_8$
Remington Model 1100	$1^3/_8$	$1^3/_4$	$14^3/_8$
Remington Model 1100, Monte Carlo	$1^3/_8$—$1^3/_8$	$1^7/_8$	$14^3/_8$
Remington Model 1100, Skeet	$1^1/_2$	$2^1/_2$	$13^7/_8$
Ithaca Model 37, Field	$1^5/_8$	$2^3/_4$	14
Ithaca Model 37, Skeet	$1^1/_2$	$3^1/_2$	14
Winchester Model 97 (obsolete since 1954)	$1^3/_4$	$2^3/_4$	$13^7/_8$

These are standard dimensions for guns that go out for over-the-counter sales and are the manufacturer's idea of what should fit the average man. Changes in dimensions may be had on guns ordered special from the factory. Standard dimensions of $1^1/_2$ x $2^1/_2$ x 14 are a good compromise. A stock so made does quite well for a man from 5 feet, 7 inches to 5 feet, 10 inches in height who wears a 32 or 33 shirt sleeve and who has a fairly full face. I am slightly over 6 feet tall, have a thin face, long neck, and square shoulders. I wear a 34 sleeve. Such a stock is too short for me and has too much drop at comb and heel. I take a stock that measures $1^1/_2$ x $2^1/_4$ x $14^1/_4$ with $1^1/_2$ inches pitch down from 26-inch barrels. A shorter man needs less length of pull. Many shooters with full faces like the Winchester Model 97 because of the greater comb drop.

19

Choke Boring in the Shotgun

THE DISCOVERY OF CHOKE as a means of controlling shotgun patterns was one of the few really revolutionary developments in the history of the scattergun. Until choke was discovered, all barrels were bored true cylinder, a straight hole all the way through, as large at the muzzle as at the breech. Anyone who has patterned a barrel that has been chopped off at the muzzle, removing all choke, knows that straight-cylinder patterns are wide, tend to be uneven, patchy, and unreliable, and generally look like a doughnut.

This tendency of the straight cylinder to scatter shot all over the landscape is a good reason for *not* chopping off shotgun barrels behind the choke. When I was a kid my grandfather gave me an old Ithaca double that had been run over by a wagon. I took it to a plumber, who amputated the damaged barrels with a hacksaw and smoothed the muzzles with a file. All choke was removed, of course, by this operation, and although the old gun was deadly at 20 yards, out at 40 yards it would scatter shot all over the side of a house.

The universal use of the straight cylinder in the old days was probably one reason for the notion, still current, that a long-barreled gun shoots "harder" than a short-barreled one. What probably happens with a true cylinder, says E. Field White, president of the Poly-Choke Co., is that the very long barrel doesn't shoot a doughnut pattern, while the short barrel does, with loss of killing power. In the short barrel, he says, the wad—not being held up momentarily by choke in the muzzle—smashes into the shot column. But in the long barrel, the shot column gets up enough momentum to outrun the wad as pressure falls off.

At any rate, choke was invented a century ago. The American version is that it was the discovery of Fred Kimble, a professional duck hunter of Illinois. But the English assert that a British patent on choke antedated Kimble's work.

In standard choke, a cone (actually, to be technically correct, a cut-off portion, or frustrum, of a cone) extends from the end of the bore to the beginning of the "parallel" or "lede." The difference between the bore diameter and the parallel diameter is the amount of constriction, which controls the patterns. It is usually measured in thousandths of an inch, also called "points." The length and slant of the cone will vary from make to make and from choke to choke, depending upon the pattern wanted. The usual rule: The wider the pattern wanted, the less the constriction and the shorter the cone and the parallel. Thus, guns designed for dense patterns and heavy shot charges tend to have long cones and parallels.

Choke, then, is the difference—constriction—between the bore diameter and the parallel diameter. Theoretically, a full choke has from 30/1000 to 40/1000 inch constriction, or to put it a more convenient way, .030 to .040 inch. Hence the term "half choke" for a modified choke of 20 points (.020 inch) constriction. Since the "standard" boring of a 12-gauge is supposed to measure .729 inch, a muzzle with .040-inch constriction should measure about .690 inch.

Not all 12-gauge barrels, however, have a bore diameter of .729. One manufacturer's specifications call for .725. And I have just measured, with an inside micrometer, three barrels from two manufacturers. One is bored .727 inch, the two others .735.

And so we have variation in bore diameters among shotguns of different makes and, to some extent, among shotguns of the same make. On top of that, full-choke patterns are often (usually, in fact, these days) produced with a lot less than .040-inch constriction. So the old notion that "If you can put a dime down the muzzle of a 12-gauge shotgun, it isn't full-choke" doesn't hold true.

Let's take a look at some figures. One full-choke barrel with a bore diameter of .727 inch comes down to .702 at the muzzle. It has .025-inch constriction, which is a long way from the theoretical .030–.040 inch of the full choke. This particular barrel is very definitely full choke, for it patterns maximum loads of No. 6 better than 70 percent. The average dime will go into it with a snug fit, and an undersized dime will go in easily; some dimes I've measured run from .701 to .703 inch. Another barrel is supposed to be bored improved modified, and its patterns range from 65 to 70 percent. It has a bore diameter of .735 and a muzzle diameter of .716—or .019-inch constriction. Here is a barrel that produces practically full-choke patterns and yet it has less than half the theoretical 40 points (.040 inch) constriction. A good horseshoe player could toss a dime down the muzzle from across the room.

Very few American full-choke barrels are given .040 inch constriction. One factory sets standard constriction for a full-choke 12-gauge at 36 points (.036 inch); another makes it .035. One prewar 12-gauge Magnum double, chambered for 3-inch shells, shoots very dense patterns—and it has .050 inch constriction. On the other hand, I had one barrel with .018 inch constriction that regularly produced patterns averaging slightly above 70 percent.

Neither is there anything to the notion that the more constriction a barrel has, the denser its pattern will be and the farther it will kill. When con-

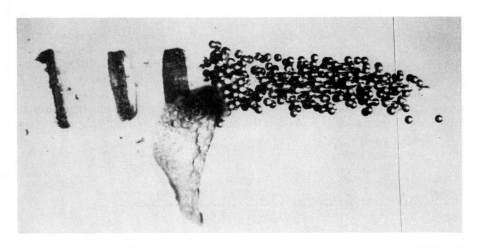

This is what shot looks like as it comes out of the barrel. The polyethylene collar that protects the shot is falling off.

striction is increased beyond a certain point, pattern density falls off. In the process of manufacture and testing, pattern density is often improved by "relieving" the choke, which means removing some of the constriction. I once had a Model 12 Winchester equipped with a Poly-Choke. Set at modified, the gadget would give full-choke patterns that would knock your eye out. Closed up more, the patterns began to fall off. The man who patterns a gun equipped with such a device and who opens it up to obtain denser patterns is doing exactly what the barrel man at the factory does when he relieves the choke with a reamer.

Ordinarily, though, we can say that the constriction of a full-choke 12-gauge is *supposed* to run from .030 to .040 inch, with an average of perhaps .035. Modified or half-choke boring will have a constriction of from .015 to .020 inch, and should produce patterns of 55–60 percent. Improved cylinder boring in this country means a constriction of .006 to .010 inch, with patterns running 40–50 percent.

Besides the three standard chokes (full, modified, and improved cylinder) one often hears of "improved modified," which is supposed to pattern about 65 percent, and "quarter choke," a strong improved cylinder which has about .010 inch constriction and which is supposed to pattern 50–55 percent, putting it right on the heels of the modified boring. Actually this strong improved cylinder, or quarter choke, is excellent for the average shot. I have a double with .011 inch constriction in the right barrel and .013 in the left; it gives beautiful patterns, averaging about 50 percent right and 55 percent left, with almost anything I feed it.

For the most part the gun companies are pretty leery about handing out precise data on their chokes or degrees of constriction. Such dope leads to a lot of grief, because the average man is likely to judge his gun by the hole in the barrel and not by the patterns it shoots. The amount of constriction is a means to an end—*not* an end in itself. The final test of a gun is the pattern it produces. If a particular boring puts 70 percent or more of a load of shot into a 30-inch circle at 40 yards, the gun is giving full-choke performance, whether it has .012 inch constriction or .040. With the new-type wads and wadless crimps used in our excellent modern ammunition, full-choke patterns are produced with far less constriction than was necessary with old-type ammunition—at least, that is what my pattern board tells me.

In *general,* though, the following table (although there has been much deviation from it) was accepted in the past as standard for 12 gauge guns by gunmakers:

Boring (choke)	Constriction (inches)	Shot in 30-inch circle at 40 yards (percent)
Full	.040	70
Three-quarter (improved-modified)	.030	65
Half (modified)	.020	60
Quarter	.010	55
Improved cylinder	.003–.009	50
Cylinder	None	35–40

This business of the percentage of shot in a 30-inch circle at 40 yards is pretty much of an abstraction. More useful and to the point is the knowledge of what sort of patterns we are working with at actual game ranges, for at least 90 percent of all game killed is taken *at less than* 40 yards.

What then? Let's take a look at Major Gerald Burrard's great book *The Modern Shotgun.* It deals with British guns but the dope is applicable to ours, too. He gives us the following table, showing the spread of the pattern according to choke and at various ranges:

Range, (yards)	Pattern spread (inches)			
	Cyl.	Imp. cyl.	Mod.	Full
10	19	15	12	9
15	26	20	16	12
20	32	26	20	1
25	38	32	26	21
30	44	38	32	26
35	51	44	38	32
40	57	51	46	40

Suppose we take 25 yards as the average range at which upland game is killed and then glance at the table. We see that it would probably be a lot easier to hit a bird with the 32-inch pattern thrown by an improved-cylinder boring than with the 21-inch pattern thrown by a full choke.

Actually, I am convinced that American guns and modern American ammunition will average even smaller patterns than those above. For example, the British standard for the improved cylinder runs from .003 to .005 inch constriction, whereas the American standard apparently runs from .005 to .010. A fine double of mine was presumably bored improved cylinder in both barrels, but actually it had about .015 inch constriction. With either skeet or trap loads it patterned around 70 percent, and at 20 yards, each barrel threw a killing pattern of just about 16 inches.

The standard methods of achieving choke are by no means universal. For many years it has been common practice to swage down the muzzles of inexpensive guns to impart some degree of choke. The method works, too.

One famous gun factory makes all its chokes without parallels. The chokes are cone-shaped and cut to various degrees with the same reamer; it is simply run in deeper for an improved cylinder than for a full choke. This leads one to question the utility of the parallel at the muzzle.

Still another type is the "recess" or "jug" choke. I do not believe it has been adopted by any manufacturer, but it is used by gunsmiths to give

Pattern shapes like this are handy for patterning a shotgun and determining the effectiveness of the load.

some degree of choke to a barrel after its muzzle end and constriction have been cut off. These recesses are from 1 inch to 6 inches long, from .003 to .008 inch deep, and begin about $^1/_2$ inch from the muzzle. A friend of mine cut a recess into the barrel of an old pump gun (it had lost a few inches of muzzle) by using emery cloth on the end of a rod. It was a rough-and-ready process, but the jug he made rounded up his patterns and brought them up to about 50 percent.

The wildfowl hunter whose specialty is pass shooting wants all the choke—all the pattern density at long range—he can get. But for many types of shooting the exact opposite is true; then the man behind the gun wants all the *spread* he can get. Bobwhite quail in brush are shot fast at close range. So are woodcock and ruffed grouse. With much choke, game like that is either missed cold, or badly mutilated. For that matter, the humble cottontail, darting from brush patch to brush patch, is often shot at very close range, and the greater the spread you have then the better.

Canny upland hunters have always demanded a lot of spread at short ranges, but it was the game of skeet that really gave the wide-open chokes a boost.

At the start, it was shot with ordinary double guns, bored improved cylinder and modified. Then some unknown genius sawed his barrels off to get straight-cylinder patterns. That gave him an edge. The next step was an attempt to get patterns wider than improved cylinder, since skeet targets are broken at between 20 and 25 yards. One way to lick the problem is to give a skeet barrel a "bell" or "reverse" choke.

Some special skeet guns have one variety or another of this bell choke, usually under a mysterious name like Skeet No. 1, Skeet No. 2, or Skeet In and Skeet Out. Skeet No. 1, or Skeet In, is designed to throw as wide a pattern as possible for the incoming bird, and will pattern 35-40 percent in a 30-inch circle at 40 yards. Skeet No. 2, or Skeet Out, is for the outgoing bird that the slower shooter takes at greater range. However, the good fast shooter will break all his targets over Station 8, so he wants all the pattern he can get. As a result the closer Skeet No. 2 boring is not popular.

Skeet No. 1 is a variety of the bell choke and No. 2 simply a conventional standard choke with .015 inch constriction; it will usually throw a weak modified (or about 55 percent) pattern. Skeet No. 2 is an excellent choke for the longer shots at upland game but the patterns are pretty small for the man who busts his birds over Station 8.

Actually Skeet No. 1 is a pretty fair boring for upland shooting, and its wide patterns will make the man of average skill look good. Many years ago, I got myself a double gun with two sets of barrels—one set bored Skeet No. 1 and No. 2, the other modified and full. First day of the dove season, I thought I'd try the skeet barrels for a few shots. I planned to replace them with the more closely choked barrels if I found myself feathering many birds. I don't believe I shot at a bird at more than 30 yards, but I killed ten with twelve shots and didn't lose a cripple. Eight of the birds were killed with the No. 1 boring.

Still another time I was in Mexico with some friends on a deer hunt, and had along as a pot gun a 20-gauge fitted with a Weaver-Choke. I put the skeet tube on it and killed ten straight doves as they came in over a cottonwood tree, range about 20 or 25 yards. I doubt that I could have done any such shooting with a modified barrel and know I couldn't with a full choke.

During the upland-game season one year my wife used a 16-gauge Winchester skeet gun bored Skeet No. 1 and No. 2, whereas I used a double which was supposed to be bored improved cylinder in both barrels but actually gave patterns averaging between improved modified and full. My wife almost never had to chase a cripple, while I did now and then. The reason, I believe, is that she was hitting them with more shot, because of wide patterns, while I was catching too many birds on the edge of my small one. Of course, beyond 30 yards Skeet No. 1 boring, as well as the various skeet and short-range tubes of the variable-choke devices, throw patterns too thin to be effective and should not be used. However, most upland game is shot at less than 30 yards. The same thing applies to the light improved cylinders with .003–.005 inch constriction.

Light-constriction or reverse chokes are special-purpose jobs, and the same thing can be said of the heavy chokes with .035 to .040-inch constriction. They are just about as worthless for 15–25-yard upland shooting as the reverse chokes and open improved-cylinders are for pass shooting at 45–65 yards.

The most useful degrees of choke run from .007 to .017 inch of constriction and give patterns ranging from 50 to 60 percent in a 30-inch circle at 40 yards. Most barrels so bored will produce fair patterns with practically any size of shot from No. 9 to No. 4, and almost any sort of load. They throw patterns relatively easy to hit with at 25 yards, yet are deadly at 40. These degrees of constriction apply, of course, to the 12-gauge. Smaller gauges need less constriction to obtain similar results—the smaller the gauge the less the constriction.

As we have seen there are several methods of obtaining desired patterns. What counts is *not* the type of choke, the degree of constriction, the length of cone, or anything else. What counts is *pattern!*

Indicated choke, as stamped on the barrel, doesn't mean too much; one maker's cylinder is another's improved cylinder; another's improved modified is still another one's full. One company will consider a gun that patterns 50 percent to be improved cylinder, whereas a competitor would call it modified. In my experience almost all guns pattern more densely with the new-type shells than one would expect from the markings on the barrel.

The way to evaluate a choke is *not* to measure it (as I have done in this chapter), not to try to ram a dime into the muzzle, but to find out what percentage of the shot charge it will put into a 30-inch circle at the ranges you will usually run into in the hunting field.

Names don't mean much. Neither does degree of constriction. What *does* count is the size of the pattern and the distribution of the shot in it. Gamebirds aren't killed with names. They are killed with good, effective patterns!

The following table shows the approximate amount of constriction used, by one concern, at the muzzle to give the several well-known degrees of choke boring.

**AMOUNT OF CONSTRICTION AT MUZZLE
FOR DIFFERENT CHOKE BORINGS**

Gauge	Boring	Bore Diam.	Muzzle Diam.	Constriction	Percent at 40 yards In 30-inch circle
10	Full choke	.775	.740	.035	70
	Modified choke	.775	.758	.017	60
	Imp. cylinder	.775	.768	.007	50
	Cylinder	.775	.775	None	40
12	Full choke	.725	.695	.030	70
	Modified choke	.725	.710	.015	60
	Imp. cylinder	.725	.719	.006	50
	Cylinder	.725	.725	None	40
16	Full choke	.662	.638	.024	70
	Modified choke	.662	.650	.012	60
	Imp. cylinder	.662	.657	.005	50
	Cylinder	.662	.662	None	40
20	Full choke	.615	.594	.021	70
	Modified choke	.615	.605	.010	60
	Imp. cylinder	.615	.611	.004	50
	Cylinder	.615	.615	None	40
28	Full Choke	.550	.533	.017	70
	Modified choke	.550	.542	.008	60
	Imp. cylinder	.550	.547	.003	50
	Cylinder	.550	.550	None	40
.410 bore*	Full choke	.410	.396	.014	70
	Modified choke	.410	.405	.005	60
	Imp. cylinder	.410	.408	.002	50
	Cylinder	.410	.410	None	40

*Percentages obtained at 25 yards.

20

This Stuff Called Shot

BECAUSE SO FEW GUNNERS ever shoot at anything with a smoothbore unless it has hair or feathers on it, the whole subject of shot has a good deal of folklore conneected with it. One chap I know hunts grouse with No. 4s and claims the big shot smashes through brush and twigs better than any smaller shot. Another uses No. 9 on grouse and claims the smaller shot, because there are more of them, get through the holes in the foliage. Both stunts sound logical, and both kill grouse. So far as I know, neither has ever put up paper behind some foliage to find out which was right.

Shot is made of lead because lead is heavy and relatively cheap. It is also soft and does not mar the relatively soft steel of shotgun barrels. Now and then someone removes the shot from a shell and reloads with steel air-rifle shot when he thinks he wants larger shot than is locally available. For two reasons this is a sour idea. For one thing the steel shot are less dense (weigh less for their size) than lead and lose their velocity more rapidly. For another, they are hard and often score the barrel badly.

"Soft" or "drop" shot is now obsolete. It was pure lead with a bit of arsenic added. Formerly many hunters, particularly quail hunters in the South, swore by it, as they felt that the "soft" shot expanded like an expanding bullet when it struck the bird and hence had greater killing power. Most experts believe this is an old wives' tale. It is true that an examination of a bird killed with drop shot will show a high percentage of deformed or upset pellets, but they were probably deformed by the forcing cone of the chamber or by the cone of the choke and not after they struck the bird. Drop shot throw a wider pattern because of the high percentage of deformed shot, and hence may be somewhat easier to hit with; but they pattern less reliably than harder shot and in the long run probably allow a higher proportion of cripples to get away.

"Chilled" or hard shot are hardened by the addition of antimony. Because they are harder, such shot do not give as high a percentage of

131

deformed pellets and hence throw better and more even patterns. They also lead the barrel less, and they produce a shorter shot string because of less shot deformity. Chilled shot is now standard.

Still harder, still less liable both to deformation and to the leading of the barrel, is copperized or copper-plated shot, which is used in some premium loads.

Shot is manufactured by pouring the molten alloyed lead through pans with various-size holes in them to correspond with size of shot wanted. The streams of shot form into spheres as they fall from a tower of considerable height. They are cooled by striking water below. Then the shot is collected and the shot that is out of round is eliminated by letting all the shot run down a series of inclined planes. The round shot pellets run true, but the shot out of round run cockeyed and fall off at the side, where they are collected, remelted, and given another chance.

Besides buckshot, "birdshot" was formerly manufactured in all sizes, for No. 12 or "dust," which, I believe, is the size still loaded in .22 shotshells, through No. 10 (which many fancied for snipe) to No. 1. Through the course of the years, though, shotgun loads (combination of sizes and kinds of shot and amounts and kinds of powder in various gauges) have been trimmed down literally from thousands to less than 200 and the trimming has eliminated not only the old "soft" shot but many odd sizes. No. 9, the smallest size currently manufactured for regular gauges, is used in skeet. From then on the list goes No. 8, No. 7½, No. 6, No. 5, No. 4, No. 2, and BB.

A trick for finding the size of shot is to subtract the size from 17 and the

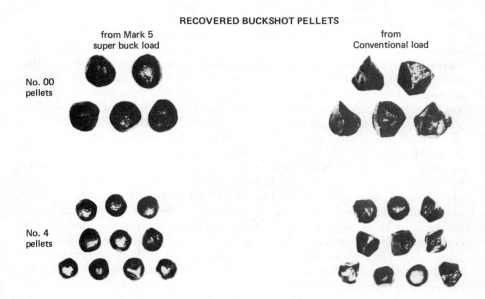

RECOVERED BUCKSHOT PELLETS

from Mark 5
super buck load

from
Conventional load

No. 00
pellets

No. 4
pellets

Conventional lead shot is soft, and it is deformed as it passes down the barrel. Modern shotshells (left) have plastic collars that protect the shot from deformation.

answer is the size in hundredths of an inch. As for instance, take No.8, subtract from 17, and the answer is .09, the size of the shot. Other sizes are as follows: No. 9–.08; No. $7^1/_2$–.095; No. 6–.11; No. 5–.12; No. 4–.13; No. 2–.15; BB–.18.

For the lads who write in and want to know how many shot of a certain size in a certain charge, here is some material for the old notebook, the number of shot per ounce: No. 2–88; No. 4–136; No. 5–172; No. 6–223; No. $7^1/_2$–343; No. 8–409; No. 9–585. One ounce is the maximum charge for the 20-gauge, of course, and the "standard" load for the 16-gauge.

For the maximum $1^1/_8$-ounce load for the load for the 16-gauge or the "standard" $1^1/_8$-ounce load for the 12-gauge figures would be as follows: No. 2–99; No. 4–153; No. 5–193; No. 6–215; No. $7^1/_2$–388; No. 8–460; No. 9–658.

For the so-called "maximum" 12-gauge load in $2^3/_4$-inch cases (Super-X, Nitro Express, Super Speed, etc.) with $1^1/_4$ ounces of shot, here's the dope: No. 2–110; No. 4–170; No. 5–215; No. 6–279; No. $7^1/_2$–431; No. 8–514; No 9–731.

These figures may vary a bit, depending on what shot tower and by what outfit they are made, but they are near enough to being exact to enable the shooter to use them in figuring pattern percentages. Suppose a sharp man with a pencil shoots his favorite musket at 40 yards, draws a circle to enclose the largest number of shot, and counts 215 holes. He has used a load containing $1^1/_4$ ounces of No. $7^1/_2$ which contains presumably about 430 shot. By spending a few minutes of hard labor and by invoking the aid of the wife and young and the cop on the corner, he will be able to deduce that he has got a 50 percent or improved-cylinder pattern. If on the other hand they had counted 323 holes, he would eventually determine that he had secured a good full-choke pattern of about 75 percent.

Everyone should pattern his shotgun with different combinations of shot size and powder charge, by the way, since for no good reason known to man, particular guns like particular shot sizes. For example we have a 20-gauge Ithaca double on the rack bored improved cylinder (right) and modified (left). That doggoned right barrel will for whatever the reason pattern one certain brand of trap loads from 65 to 70 percent, or what is called "improved modified," instead of throwing an improved-cylinder pattern of around 50 percent. Recently I had a letter from a chap with a skeet gun of a certain make. With it and another brand of trap loads, he was getting patterns of 80 percent. That doesn't seem right, but that's how the figures he sent me turned out. The duck shot may find that his gun will give denser patterns with No. 5 shot than with No. 6 or vice versa. It may shoot No. 4 shot and it may not. One season my wife shot an open-bored 16-gauge on quail with high-velocity shells with $1^1/_8$ ounces of No. $7^1/_2$. Too late she found that at 30 yards the patterns thrown by the right barrel had holes right in the middle you could throw Elizabeth Taylor through. The better she held the more certain she was to miss or feather her bird. A shift to the trap load with No. 8 shot cured it.

Almost any ammunition company catalog will contain a table of shot size recommendations like the following, which I have swiped in toto from the Western Ammunition Handbook:

FOR UPLAND SHOOTING

	Shot Sizes
Snipe, woodcock, rail, quail in early season and small shore birds	8 or 9
Dove, quail in late season, large shore birds and small winged pests	7, 7$^1/_2$ or 8
Pheasant, prairie chicken, grouse, rabbit and squirrel	4, 5, 6 or 7
Turkey and large furred vermin	BB, 2 or 4

FOR WILDFOWL SHOOTING

Duck shooting over decoys	5 or 6
All other duck shooting	4
Goose shooting	BB, 2 or 4

FOR TRAPSHOOTING

16-yard singles and first barrel of doubles	7$^1/_2$ or 8
Second barrel of doubles and handicap targets	7$^1/_2$ or 8

FOR SKEET SHOOTING

For any skeet shooting	9

Many years of experience by many very smart people have gone into the compilation of such lists, and most gunners will have no fault to find with them. However, some will. There are two principal schools of dissenters— the small-shot advocates and the big-shot advocates. One correspondent of mine, a Westerner with a lot of hunting behind him, belongs to the small-shot school and every time I mention the subject he writes a letter leaping right down my throat. He advocates the use of no shot larger than No. 7$^1/_2$, *even on geese*. On those big birds, he says, the gunner should hold far enough to center the head and neck, then the numerous little shot will get in their dirty work, with the result that there is a clean kill. He also claims that larger shot ball up in the feathers and do not penetrate as deeply as the smaller shot.

Members of the small-shot school say that birds are not killed cleanly by wounds in nonvital areas or by shock but that they are killed by hits in vital areas—the brain, the spine, the neck—and that the more shot thrown at them the better the chances are for vital hits.

The large-shot boys say that small shot quickly lose their velocity and energy and if they do not happen to hit a vital area, they do not have sufficient shock to down a bird. Instead, they say, the pellets give poor penetration, cause gangrene and slow death.

Let's take a look at a few energy figures. In the 12-gauge with the maximum load of 3$^3/_4$ drams and 1$^1/_4$ ounces of shot, a No. 2 pellet which has a muzzle velocity of 1,444 fps, has an energy of 16 foot-pounds at 10 yards; at 20 yards of 12; at 30 yards, 10; at 40 yards, 8.6; at 50 yards, 7.3; and at 60 yards, 6.5. For No. 4 shot in the same load the figures per pellet are 10 yards, 10 foot-pounds; at 20 yards, 7.5; at 30 yards, 6.1; at 40 yards, 5.1; at 50 yards, 4.4; and at 60 yards, 3.7.

With a maximum load of No. 6, the energy per pellet at 10 yards is 5.9; at 20 yards, 4.3; at 30 yards, 3.5; at 40 yards, 2.9; at 50 yards, 2.4; and at 60 yards, 2.

With the same load of No. $7^1/_2$, the energy per pellet at 10 yards is 3.6; at 20 yards, 2.65; at 30 yards, 2.05; at 40 yards, 1.7; at 50 yards, 1.38; and at 60 yards, 1.1.

In smaller gauges, which in any case turn up less velocity at the muzzle, these retained-energy figures are somewhat less. By comparison, maximum loads for the 16-gauge give the following retained energies at 60 yards: No. 4 shot, 3.5 foot-pounds; No. 6, 1.85; and No. $7^1/_2$, 1. In the 20-gauge with maximum loads figures are at the same distance: No. 4, 3.6; No. 6, 1.92; and No. $7^1/_2$, 1.06. Not any enormous difference between the gauges.

It takes no seventh son of a seventh son, with this data to go on, to dope out that one No. 2 pellet would strike a goose or a duck at 60 yards as hard as six No. $7^1/_2$ pellets. Now there are roughly four times as many No. $7^1/_2$ pellets in a load as there are No. 2s, yet at 60 yards one No. 2 pellet, instead of hitting four times as hard, hits *six* times as hard, a gain because of the larger, heavier shot of 50 percent.

At 60 yards the velocity and energy of No. $7^1/_2$ shot has fallen off so much that, in spite of good pattern density, the little shot would be relatively ineffective and even with a neck shot it is doubtful if a kill would result. Almost any hunter has had the experience of a surprise shot at geese when the birds were way out there at 60 or 70 yards. He has literally heard the small shot rattle off the feathers and has seen the geese go sailing majestically on.

Big birds like geese and turkeys can be killed and killed very dead with small shot, but only at ranges where the pattern density is enough so that hits can be counted on in the head or neck and where energy and velocity are sufficient to ensure good penetration.

Roughly, then, the effective range on big birds with small shot is just about the same as it would be on a quail, because what you are shooting at (in this case the head and upper neck area) doesn't offer much more area to hit than the body of a quail. If with No. $7^1/_2$ or No. 8 shot a certain gun will take quail at 45 yards, it will also take geese at that distance. Actually the man using a close-shooting gun and small shot *and* shooting at the heads of geese will probably get more clean kills at a range where such shooting is effective than if he were using larger shot and holding for the body.

A Magnum 10 using 2 ounces of large shot, or a Magnum 12 using 3-inch shells with $1^5/_8$ ounces of large shot, will often kill geese at 70 and sometimes 80 yards, far beyoond the range of small shot in any amount and in any gauge.

As a practical application of this velocity and energy loss, at about 125 yards No. $7^1/_2$ and No. 8 shot will rattle off the skin. Anyone who has shot in a hard-hunted dove flyway has had this happen. No. 6 will sting a little. No. 5 will hurt. I have never seen anyone shoot under these conditions with No. 4, but they might break the skin.

Changing shot sizes around is in a way like taking something out of one pocket and putting it into another. If you go to a smaller shot size you increase pattern density and increase your chances of a vital hit, but you cut down on energy delivered per pellet and at the longer ranges on total energy delivered. If you go to a larger shot size, you gain an energy delivered per pellet, probably on total energy delivered, but you lose on pattern density and cut down on your chances of making a hit in a vital area. When, as I mentioned in the beginning of this chapter, we carried No. 2s around for long shots, we were so thinning out our patterns at long range that any hit was in the nature of an act of God.

A FEW RULES ABOUT CHOICE OF SHOT SIZE

The larger the bird, the larger the shot that can be used with the assurance that the necessary four body hits can be obtained. A goose or a wild turkey will sustain the minimum of four hits from a pattern that may leave a quail or a dove unscratched.

The tighter the pattern the larger the shot that can be used. A gun throwing a good full-choke pattern with No. 4s can still put in as many hits (with more resulting energy and killing power per pellet) than a gun throwing a cylinder pattern with the smaller and more numerous No. 5s.

The larger the gauge, the larger the shot that can be used successfully. A 10-gauge Magnum can use No. 2 shot where it would be simply silly to attempt to use them in a 20-gauge, the maximum load of which is only half that of the Magnum 10.

On the other hand, all things being equal, the smaller the gauge, the smaller the shot; the smaller the bird sought, the smaller the shot; the lighter the shot charge, the smaller the shot; the more open the boring the smaller the shot.

I am pretty skeptical if one gains anything under any circumstances by using shot larger than the following in the following gauges: .410 and 28 gauge, No. $7\frac{1}{2}$; 20 gauge, No. 6; 16 gauge, No. 5; 12 gauge, No. 4; and Magnum 12 and 10 gauge, No. 2.

From experience in the field and from a lot of shooting at mail-order catalogs, magazines, and whatnot, and then counting the number of pages penetrated, I'd say that the following figures are as correct as such a thing could be, assuming that the birds shot at are of the sort the shot is ordinarily recommended for. Effective killing range of various shot sizes: No. 9, 35 yards; No. 8, 40 yards; No. $7\frac{1}{2}$, 45 yards; No. 6, 50 yards; No. 4, 60 yards; No. 2, 65 yards in a 12-gauge Magnum or 70–75 yards in a 10-gauge Magnum.

If we had to get along with only three sizes of shot, we wouldn't be too badly off with No. $7\frac{1}{2}$ for skeet, traps, and all upland shooting, even at grouse and pheasants; No. 6 for general duck shooting, optional shooting at grouse and pheasants, and for shooting at the large birds up to 50 yards; and No. 4 for pass shooting at ducks and geese in special wildfowl guns. If we had to get along with only two shot sizes, you could cut out No. 4; and if only *one* shot size was permitted, I think I'd take No. 6, although No. $7\frac{1}{2}$ wouldn't be a bad choice either.

A good rule to make is that if there is any doubt in your mind which shot size to pick, the smaller shot which patterns more densely and which gives a better chance of a vital hit should be chosen. This last season I am sure I folded more pheasants stone dead with No. $7^1/_2$ than I did with No. 6.

The man who doesn't pattern his gun with various sizes of shot and various makes of ammunition is something like the character who blithely goes out into the deer forests come autumn without ever having sighted in his rifle or who changes bullet weights and brands of ammunition with no attempt to see how it affects his sighting. Besides shooting and evaluating the conventional patterns, a very revealing stunt is to draw the profile of a quail, a duck, a pheasant or whatnot, and then shoot at it at various ranges and *count the hits.* When a particular shot size fails to average four hits at a certain range, then it is being shot beyond its killing range and the result will be a lot of cripples that are just as truly lost to other sportsmen as if they had been taken home to the frying pan!

It is interesting and revealing to find out what these simple tests will show about *your* gun. Maybe it has an affinity, say, for No. 8 shot and will not handle No. $7^1/_2$ particularly well.

Perhaps it does poorly with high-velocity loads but beautifully with standard loads. Maybe it will pattern No. 5 better than No. 4 or vice versa.

And then when you are evaluating the patterns, remember that the shotgun is a short-range weapon and that most ranges at which game is killed are grossly overestimated. When you draw that duck silhouette, for instance, take a good look at it at 50 yards, and if it doesn't seem pretty far away, I'll eat it. Now lift it 75 feet in the air and it will look twice that far away.

At 50 yards No. 4 will knock a duck for a loop. Move him closer and No. $7^1/_2$ has all the penetration you need.

I remember one citizen in the Southwest who was the hottest thing on the duck marsh that day. The way he was folding those birds up was something to amaze. He was using a Winchester Model 21 skeet gun and either No. 8 or No. 9 shot. Another chap who bore a reputation among the natives of being about as hot a duck shot as haunted the marshes along the Pee Dee River did his shooting with a Sauer double bored improved cylinder in both barrels and he used No. 8 shot. The secret of his success was that he never shot at a bird over 35 yards away.

STEEL SHOT

For some years a controversy has been raging in the sporting press about a federal regulation requiring the use of steel shot in certain federally controlled waters. Arguments for the use of mild steel rather than lead are that lead shot that falls on certain bypes of bottom in shallow water are picked up by feeding puddle ducks (mallards, teal, etc.) and that many of the ducks eventually die from lead poisoning. Steel shot would have no such effect and would eventually rust away. Those who would substitute steel for lead for all duck hunting say that the lives of many thousands of ducks would be saved annually.

Those who are against the steel shot say it is ballistically less efficient because it takes a No. 4 steel pellet to weigh the same as a No. 6 lead pellet, that the steel shot lose their velocity more quickly and as a result wound more ducks than they save. They also say that steel shot ruin the barrels of shotguns. Those who favor steel retort that steel shot, because they are hard and do not deform, throw denser patterns with shorter shot strings than do lead shot. This would tend to reduce crippling of ducks. They also say that the shorter shot string would likewise reduce crippling and the fact that steel loses its velocity quicker would also result in fewer cripples. They say that the use of steel shot results only in a very minor ring bulge at the point where the shot charge enters the choke near the muzzle, and that the chokes do not "shoot out."

I am inclined to string along with those who advocate steel shot. I have a few fine European double guns. I would not want to take the chance of injuring their barrels with steel shot, but I would not have the slightest hesitation with a stout American-made repeater.

21

Styles in Shotgun Shooting

MANY YEARS AGO I read a piece of advice by a famous writer on shotguns and shotgun shooting. There was only one way to shoot a shotgun, he wrote. That was to look at what you wanted to hit. Then you threw the gun to the shoulder and fired the instant the butt touched the shoulder. Anyone who shot a scattergun any other way was, he assured his readers, a slow and fumbling fellow to be sneered at by all right-thinking sportsmen.

I was horrified. *I* didn't shoot a shotgun like that, I knew. I was just a self-taught slob, I realized, and my shotgun manners and form were the equivalent of drinking coffee out of a saucer and eating peas with a knife. So when the quail season came along I started keeping my eyes on my birds, paying no attention to my gun barrels, and shooting the instant the butt touched my shoulder. I also started missing. I missed and missed and missed. After a couple of weeks of it, I decided that a country boy like me better take a look at his gun barrels in relation to the bird before he touched off. Then I started hitting.

I don't know of anything that people kid themselves about more than they do about shotgun shooting. Perhaps my shotgun writer never paid any attention to the barrels and maybe he did fire the instant the butt touched his shoulder. Chances are, though, that he just *thought* he did. And that is something else.

It is wonderfully easy for the man shooting a shotgun to forget what he does. He is moseying innocently along when all of a sudden his springer spaniel dives into a little patch of grass and a cock pheasant with a tail 9 feet long and colored like seven rainbows comes threshing out cackling like a fiend from hell. The fearful apparition and the dreadful noise practically scare the pants off our hero, but somehow he manages to knock the bird down with one of the three shots in his autoloader.

Did he shoot at him, below him, to the port or to the starboard? He doesn't know. Presently he forgets that he took three shots to get that bird,

139

and that if it hadn't been for his springer he never would have got it since it wobbled off with its legs dangling and lit in some brush on the other side of the hill, where the dog finally found it. During the day he picks up two other birds for the three-bird limit. He does not have anyone to keep score on him and he doesn't count his shells. If anyone told him that he had about the same average on birds as he had on clay targets he wouldn't believe him and he would hate him for life. Even sober men and good shots forget their misses and remember their hits.

Once on a dove flight I asked ten of my amigos to keep track of their expenditure of shotgun shells in relation to the actual number of birds they picked up. Five of them were excellent shots with a lot of field, skeet, and trap experience. The other five were run-of-the -mill scattergunners who maybe shot at game ten or fifteen days a year. The good shots averaged 1

THREE WAYS TO HIT MOVING TARGETS

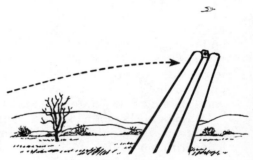

1. Snapshot Aim at point bird will be when shot charge arrives. Also called spot shot.

2. Fast Swing Start swinging from behind bird, track through it, fire when barrel is right distance ahead, with gun still moving rapidly. This technique is also called swinging past.

3. Sustained Lead Aim at point ahead of bird, moving barrel at same speed as target for long enough time to judge that gun is traveling as fast as bird. Fire with gun still swinging. Also called pointing out.

bird to 3 shells expended, the bum shots, about 1 to 9. Both good and bum shots swore that in all their lives they had never done such lousy shooting. Maybe this was because never before had they kept accurate count of their shell-to-bird ratios.

There are three ways of hitting moving objects with a shotgun—spot or "snap" shooting, the sustained lead of "pointing out" and swinging through, or, as it is also called, the fast swing. Not long ago, I read that all good shotgun shots made all their shots by the fast-swing method and those who did not use it always were a slow and dismal bunch who never really learned to shoot. I think our boy is as wrong as the chap who wrote that he never saw his gun barrels and fired the moment the butt touched his shoulder. If the truth were known I think it would be discovered that *all* good shots employ all three methods. Under some conditions the fast swing is the best, under some the spot shot. All three types of shooting are used by the field shot at moving game. Each has its advantages.

But first let us define our terms. By snap shooting or spot shooting we mean firing at the place where we hope the bird or target will be when the shot charge arrives. We do not swing our gun. If the lead does not amount to much, this is the best and surest way of hitting something with either a rifle or a shotgun. It is also the fastest way to get off a shot. It is a method widely employed by woodcock and grouse hunters who must of necessity shoot very fast and simply throw their shot charges at a point where they hope they will intercept the flight of the birds. Likewise it is the way to shoot with a rifle at a charging lion, which case you would "lead" by holding a bit low. It is also the way to shoot at a deer or sheep climbing out of a canyon and quartering away—by holding a bit high and to one side. When I shoot skeet I spot-shot one target—the No. 1 high-house bird, which is an outgoer, From the No. 1 station the bird is going directly away and dropping rapidly. If the gunner shoots right at it, he'll miss it. He has the choice then of swinging rapidly down with it (fast swing) or simply shooting a foot or a foot and a half under it with a stationary gun. That's what I do—and so do many other skeet shooters.

For anything other than a fairly gentle angel, spot shooting is no good with either a shotgun or a rifle. If anyone doesn't believe that, all he has to do is to try to shoot a round of skeet by shooting where he thinks they'll be. He'll find out many strange things on those targets whose flights approach a right angle—principally that he can't hit them.

If the flight of a game bird or a clay target is anything except a very easy angle, some other method other than spot shooting must be employed —either the fast swing (swinging past) or the sustained lead (pointing out). When the fast swing is employed the gunner starts with the muzzle behind the bird, swings his gun apparently faster than the bird is moving and fires when he thinks the muzzle is the proper distance ahead *with the muzzle still moving faster than the bird.*

This is a good way to shoot crossing birds, and many of the best shots use it for almost any angled target. It is a fine method for the upland gunner, who usually must shoot quickly, even on a crossing bird. It is almost but not quite as fast as spot shooting, and if there is much angle to the shot it is far more reliable.

This method of fast swing or swinging past is the one used by almost all trap shooters. They get the line on the bird's flight by starting behind it as it shoots out of the house, tracking past it, swinging rapidly, and then firing when they think the barrel is the right distance ahead with the gun still moving rapidly. Naturally the trap shooter has to swing farther ahead for a sharply angled target than for a straightaway or quartering shot.

The fast swing is also the method used by most good skeet shots. They pick up the bird 10 feet or so out of the trap house, swing rapidly, and fire when the muzzle gets ahead. The fast swinger usually breaks his birds before they get to Station 8 in the middle of the field. The faster a man swings, the less he has to lead, and the slower his reaction time is, the less he has to lead. Often a fine shot will swear that he doesn't lead a trap or skeet target at all but fires the instant he catches up with the clay and sees it over his gun barrel. That is, of course, a physical impossibility. Any moving object must be led if it is to be hit.

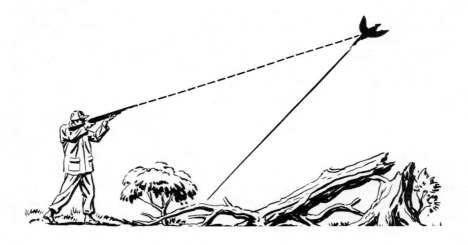

A pheasant usually rises sharply and if the hunter shoots fast with an open-bore, high-shooting upland gun, he'll probably connect.

Answer is, of course, that no one fires the instant his brain tells him to fire. When the proper sight picture registers in his brain, he decides to shoot. It takes an appreciable interval, though, for the message to pass from his brain to his finger, then for his finger to press the trigger, the primer to ignite, the powder to burn, and the shot charge to pass up the bore. All this time his gun barrel is traveling ahead. Some men react faster than others. If the man who swings fast has a slow reaction time, he is giving his birds a lot of lead without knowing it.

With any sort of swing, what is one man's lead is another's poison. Of two very good skeet shots of my acquaintance, one says he leads the No. 4 and No. 5 high-house birds, which are traveling at approximately right angles and which, like any skeet targets, leave the trap at 60 miles an hour "about

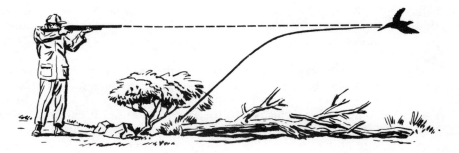

This is a true, though seldom seen, straightaway shot that calls for a dead-on hold.

4 or 5 feet," which would be about what I try to lead them. The other guy claims he never leads skeet targets, always shoots right at them. Curiously the chap who says he leads them 4 or 5 feet is the faster swinger and faster shot, the type of gunner who sees things so fast that he can walk halfway to the No. 1 high house from the No. 8 station and still powder the targets.

When the gunner has plenty of time and wants the utmost precision, the best method is, to my own way of thinking, the sustained lead—or "pointing out" as it is sometimes called. With this method the gunner keeps the muzzle of his weapon a certain distance ahead of his target for a long enough time to enable him to tell his gun is traveling apparently as fast as the bird. Then he fires with the gun still swinging.

This method is the one used by most pass shooters at ducks or at doves. It does not need to be an interminable swing, as the sustained leader needs only to maintain his lead long enough for him to be sure it is what he con-

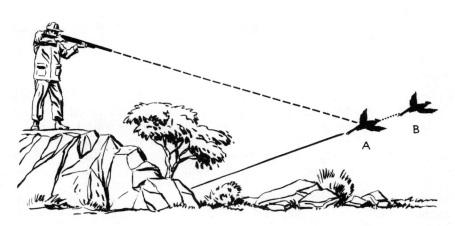

When a bird flushes from below, many hunters think it is a straightaway shot and aim at A. The bird will be at B when the shot arrives.

siders right. Bill Weaver, the scope manufacturer, who is one of the best shotgun shots I know, says he takes every passing bird with the sustained lead. He is a very quick shot, a guy whom I once saw make a triple of Hungarian partridges.

In a way the sustained lead is self-correcting, as the faster the target is moving, the faster the gunner has to swing to stay ahead. Hence he is swinging a lot faster on a fast bird than on a slow one and is hence in actuality "leading" more. This is also the method to use on running game, particularly on plains game like the American pronghorn antelope or the many African and Asiatic plains species and on deer in the open country where they are often found. Once I used this method a great deal on running jackrabbits and coyotes and I often surprised myself at how many jacks I'd hit. In the semi-open canyon country of the West, both mule and whitetail deer are often shot as they pick them up and lay them down and most good running shots like the sustained-lead method.

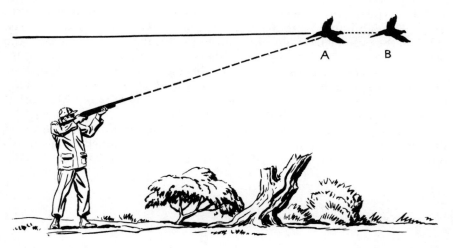

This shot would seem to call for a dead-on hold, but actually the bird is at an angle. The hunter should hold at B.

Although many good shotgun shots may forget exactly what they do in the heat of battle, I think it is highly probable that most of them in the course of a day's hunt use all three methods, even though they do not realize it and might deny it. When I hunt quail and pheasants I use rather straight-stocked guns that tend to shoot high. For that one purpose they have a bit of built-in lead. Consequently I'll shoot right at a jumping pheasant. Likewise I spot shoot if he is quartering, as then I'll hold a bit to one side and possibly a hair high. If my birds are in brush or crossing at short range, I naturally use the fast swing. But let us suppose that someone has put up a chink rooster from a hill above me and he is coming down past 40 yards away so fast I can see him rip through the air like a jet plane. Then I use the sustained lead and hope for the best.

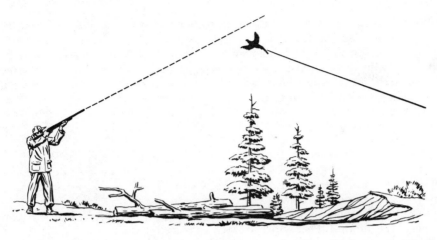

The natural instinct to want to see what you are shooting at may cause you to hold dead-on an overhead, incoming bird. Actually, you should lead as shown here with a rapidly swinging gun.

Just because a man is a fine shotgun handler it is no sign that he is necessarily a good man to consult about shooting or one whose word should be taken as gospel. Good shotgun shooting is done with the eyes, the muscles, the reflexes, not necessarily with the brain—although that helps too. Often fine performers are poor coaches, and indifferent performers are fine coaches. This goes for shotgun shooting as well as for tennis, golf, football, or any other sport.

There are various styles of shooting, then and all of them are useful in special conditions. Those who hunt in heavy cover will do a lot of spot shooting or snap shooting, call it what you will. The pass shooter will tend to use the sustained lead, and the more methodical and scientific shooters

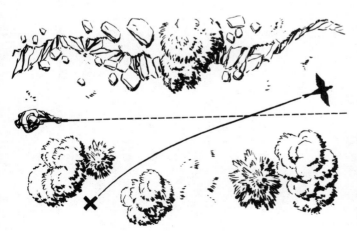

It is important to lead a bird flushed at X and flying off at a slight angle. Thinking he has a straightaway shot, the hunter in this drawing holds dead-on—and misses.

will also tend toward it. The upland gunner will do a lot of spot shooting and he'll also use the fast swing.

But whatever method of shooting he uses, he has to see his gun barrel in relation to his bird when the shot goes off. Doing that with the shotgun is precisely the same thing as calling the shot with a rifle, and no one ever became a good shot without this ability to call them. Our shotgun shooter may be so expert, so automatic, that he is able to dismiss from his mend this target-to-gun barrel picture. He may even forget that he saw it, but if he is a good shot he has to see it.

And no matter whether he uses the fast swing or the sustained lead he has to keep that gun swinging. If he slows it or stops it, he is sunk, no matter what method he uses. Likewise he is sunk if he doesn't keep his face down on the comb of the stock.

Next time you go afield with the old smoothbore, keep track of the way you actually shoot. I'll bet you a cookie you use all three methods. Also keep track of the number of birds you bring home for the shells you expend. I'll bet another cookie you'll be surprised at how many you use. I usually am.

22

Beginning with a Handgun

WHEN THE AVERAGE AMERICAN picks up a handgun and attempts to fire a shot he is about as much at home with it as he would be with a pair of chopsticks. Usually he couldn't hit the southern exposure of a northbound elephant at 30 yards. How come?

Possibly it's the influence of horse operas American kids have been seeing for the past 50 years. Unconsciously the impressionable lads absorb the technique of movie revolver shooting and imitate it. The heroes and likewise the villains grasp the pistola far over to the side. Before they cut a shot loose, they bring their revolvers back as far as the right ear. Then throw them forward in the general direction of what they plan to hit. Bang! go the revolvers. Down go the redskins, the villains, or whatever they are shooting at.

All this is excellent entertainment. The movements are fluid, the effect dramatic; but as a system of shooting a handgun it is enough to make a strong man wring his hands in anguish. The young moviegoers eat it up, not realizing that what they are seeing is not handgun shooting at all but instead a formal figure in a ballet. Watch a group of children playing cowboys and Indians some day and you'll find they handle their cap pistols just like the cowboys in the oat operas. Then when the time comes for them to shoot a real sure-enough handgun, they try their cap-pistol technique and can't hit anything. Often their beginning interest in handguns is killed because of their initial failures.

It is true that the handgun is the most difficult of all firearms to learn to shoot well, but if anyone starts right it isn't nearly as difficult as many believe. The lad who gets a suitable handgun, who starts using good form, and who practices will be shooting well before he knows it.

What sort of a handgun should the beginner select to start out with? The first fairly serious handgun shooting I ever did was with, of all things, a .38

Special, but I wouldn't advise most beginners to tee off with a gun having that much blast and recoil. I do not think there is much argument but that the beginner's gun should be a .22. The little rimfire cartridge has many advantages. It is inexpensive, and can be obtained about anywhere in the world that ammunition is sold. But even more important is the fact that the .22 has a mild report and very little recoil. As we shall see, this is of prime importance, since flinching and yanking the trigger are the major reasons for poor handgun shooting.

What type should this .22 be, automatic or revolver? You have me there! For whatever the reason, I shoot somewhat better with a revolver than I do with an automatic. Possibly that's just one of my oddball notions, like my notion that I can do better shooting out in the field with a double-barrel shotgun than I can with a pump or automatic. Actually a very high percentage of crack handgun shots prefer the automatic because of its superiority in timed and rapid fire. Probably the revolver is somewhat *safer* because it is so much easier to see quickly if the weapon is loaded or not. The revolver also has the advantage of being able to handle .22 Shorts, Longs, or Long Rifle cartridges as the shooter chooses.

The best handgun to start with is the .22, which is available in many styles and price ranges. At top left is the Colt Officer's Model target revolver, and next to it is the Smith & Wesson K-22. Both have adjustable sights. The other revolver is a Harrington & Richardson Model 999, moderately priced and accurate. The autoloaders are the Ruger Mark 1 at far left, the High Standard Sport King below it, and in the center the Colt Sport Model Woodsman with 4½-inch barrel.

The author, about to let off a shot with a revolver here, found he did better shooting with a revolver than with an automatic.

On the other hand, a .22 automatic with a fairly short barrel and good sights is an excellent supplementary weapon for the sportsman—short, flat, more convenient to carry than the bulkier revolver. The .22 automatic is a fine little weapon to pick up small game with, probably better than the revolver. Often I have seen grouse sit in a tree while a man with an automatic missed three or four times. The birds seem frightened less by the noise than they do by the movement of the shooter's thumb in the recocking of the revolver. Run-of-the-mine handgun shot though I am, I have eaten a lot of grouse and rabbits that I have plucked off with handguns. They tasted nice indeed. On one abortive sheep and elk hunt when my companions and I didn't get any real meat until the trip was almost over, we would have had to live on pancakes and oatmeal if one of my companions hadn't taken along a Colt Woodsman. As it was, we very largely subsisted on blue grouse and biscuits—and biscuits are a lot better with blue grouse than they are without. A rugged character I knew once walked 600 miles across the mountains and tundra of the subarctic in the dead of winter on snowshoes with a Hudson Bay blanket and a Smith & Wesson .22 target revolver. Mostly he ate ptarmigan and snowshoe rabbits, but he also killed a Dall sheep and four caribou with that little handgun.

Whatever sort of a .22 our beginner selects, though, it should have adjustable sights. It is often said that no one can do an exact job of sighting in a rifle for another. It is even more true of a handgun. A revolver that is laying them in the middle of a 10-ring for one shooter may be clear out of the black for another. People see their sights differently. They hold differently. Because of different ways of holding, the handgun recoils differently and gives an entirely different point of impact. The same gun will shoot two different bullet weights to different points of impact and the same bullet at different velocities to different points of impact.

Nonadjustable sights are all right for close-range self-defense and military work, but the person who wants to do target shooting, who wants to knock over small game, or who wants to astonish the girl friend by making a tin can roll along the ground at a respectable distance wants a handgun sighted so precisely that he can hit a fairly small mark.

For target shooting, the common practice is to sight in a handgun with what is known as the "6 o'clock hold." Aim is taken at the bottom of the bullseye, so that a thin white line can be seen between the top of the front sight and the bottom of the bull. The sights are then adjusted so that the bullet strikes in the center of the bull. Such a system is by no means universal even among competitive target shots. Some of the very best hold right into the bull—or sight in to put the bullet right where the top of the front sight rests. This is the way the plinker, tin-can roller, and small-game shooter should sight in, since obviously it would be fatal to have the bullet striking 3 inches high at 25 yards, let us say.

As in most shooting, tenseness on the part of the handgun shot is probably the principal enemy of precision. Take a look at a crack shot and he usually looks at ease, relaxed, almost sloppy. If he is going to be a topflight shooter he has to be, since tense muscles produce tremors and tremors make for poor shooting.

The first step then in learning to handle a handgun is to take an easy relaxed stance with the weight distributed evenly on both feet. Most good shots face half away from the target. I have seen many, though, who face the target and some who face away from the target at a right angle. The main thing is to feel comfortable and relaxed. The left hand can be put in the trousers pocket, hooked in the belt—anywhere so it feels natural.

The one-hand target grip should be relaxed but balanced and secure. The shooter should have the feeling of holding the gun with the pad of muscles at the base of his thumb while the gun rests on his fourth finger. He will squeeze off the shot with the end of his index finger, somewhere between the last joint and tip.

The handgun itself should be an extension of the arm, and a line drawn from the point of the shoulder to the V formed by the thumb and trigger finger should pass right through the sights. The arm, of course, should be straight, not bent.

The shooter should have a feeling of holding the gun with the pad of muscles at the base of his thumb and behind the large joint of his trigger finger while the gun rests on his fourth finger. If he does this and gets this feel, he should be grasping his handgun lightly but firmly. Depending on the size of his hand and length of his index finger, he will squeeze off his shot with the end of his index finger, somewhere between the last joint and the tip. He will *not* stick his whole finger through and squeeze with the second joint as the cowboys in the horse operas do. His object is to hit something and not simply to make a noise and look picturesque.

Holding a fairly heavy handgun out at the end of a straight arm is not the easiest or most natural thing in the world, and anyone who wants to become a fairly good handgun shot can well practice strengthening those muscles. He can do dry firing, of which more later, or he can hold a milk bottle at full length.

The ideal way to learn to shoot a handgun would be to go through a course of dry firing for a couple of weeks before buying any powder. Possibly that is asking too much, because beginners like noise and action. However, 75 percent of what can be learned by actual shooting can also be learned cheaper and easier by dry firing.

Most accurate handgun sights are of the Patridge type, with square notch in the rear sight and square blade front sight. With such sights elevation is controlled by seeing that the front sight is on the level with the rear sight and windage by seeing that the front sight is in the middle of the square cut of the rear sight—by seeing the same amount of light on each side of the front sight.

Good shotgun shots see the end of the barrel only vaguely. Instead they concentrate on the bird or clay target they are trying to hit. The handgun shot is exactly the opposite. If he is to hit much he must pay more attention to his sights than he does to his target. Actually very high scores have been fired by turning the paper around and aligning the sights simply on the middle of the target. The bull's-eye would not be seen at all, yet in many cases scores would be better than the same shooter could fire by aiming at the bull! *It is absolutely fatal to let the target distract the shooter's attention from his sights!*

The beginner with the handgun is shocked and disillusioned when he discovers that he cannot hold his weapon still. Instead the doggoned front sight wiggles around in a manner to drive one nuts. Unless he is carefully coached or has read and followed some sort of elementary instructions like these, he almost always falls into the bad habit of trying to grab off a bull when the sights look just right. He thus gets into the habit of trigger jerking—and no trigger jerker can ever hit much with a handgun.

There is but one way for anyone to begin shooting a handgun and that is to keep the sights looking as good as possible and then to keep increasing pressure on the trigger until the gun goes off. Anyone who can get that through his noggin and who has enough will power to practice it is already

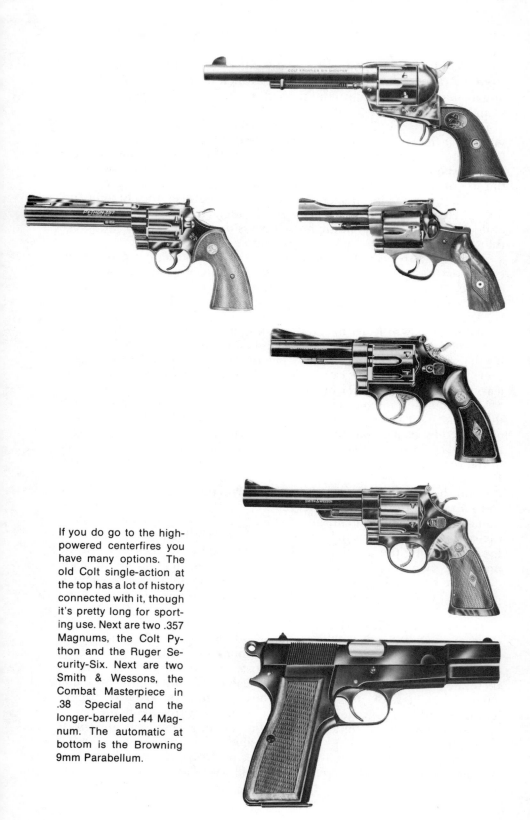

If you do go to the high-powered centerfires you have many options. The old Colt single-action at the top has a lot of history connected with it, though it's pretty long for sporting use. Next are two .357 Magnums, the Colt Python and the Ruger Security-Six. Next are two Smith & Wessons, the Combat Masterpiece in .38 Special and the longer-barreled .44 Magnum. The automatic at bottom is the Browning 9mm Parabellum.

a pretty good shot. *The wild shots come not because one cannot hold the gun steady but because of jerks and flinches.*

The handgun shooter must concentrate on his sight picture, squeeze easily and steadily, and forget when the gun is going off. If he does that he can rapidly become a pretty good handgun shot.

I am just a catch-as-catch-can handgun shot. There is absolutely but one way for me to do fairly well with any handgun—and that's it. When I begin to think about when the gun is going off, I am sunk. If I ever try to catch 10 as it rides by I am likewise sunk. I have *got* to let the gun go off by itself.

But what about genuinely good handgun shots? One told me that he knew just about when his gun was going off. Another told me he knew exactly when his gun was going off. Another assured me that he could hold his handgun rock-steady for a moment while he squeezed. But no matter what the hotshots say, the average shooter becomes pretty good only by being relaxed and comfortable, by paying more attention to his sight picture than he does to the target, and by squeezing and forgetting that his gun is ever going to go off. This business of steady holding takes care of itself, as the longer one practices, the more one shoots, the more nearly steady he can hold a handgun. He never will hold it absolutely steady and should not expect to.

The man who starts right with a handgun and does not form a lot of bad habits he has to break is lucky indeed. The man who knows how to stand, who holds his handgun properly, and who has learned to relax, who knows the sight pictures is all important, and who has convinced himself that the way to shoot properly is to keep squeezing and let the hold take care of itself is already a better shot than the average casual plinker. Then with a moderate amount of practice, this person will soon become good.

To some people accurate shooting with a handgun becomes a genuine challenge simply because it is the most difficult of all shooting skills to master. The shotgun shooter can give quite a flinch and the spread of the pattern will cover up for him. Flinching is much more serious with a rifle, but the great weight and inertia of the rifle cut down the penalties for flinching and jerking the trigger, although at that they are serious enough. With the handgun, jerking and flinching are absolutely fatal.

Not long ago I was amusing myself by shooting from 50 yards at clay trap targets set up in a sandbank with a .44 Special. Of course, I missed a lot, but when I hit one I got a genuine thrill of achievement. Even greater was my feeling of satisfaction because I didn't ever miss one very far. Another time I had a Smith & Wesson K-22 with me on a big game hunt. One night we were on a jack camp, reduced to flour, butter, jam, and a few cans of vegetables. We had a 20-gauge shotgun along for grouse but that day we were afraid of the noise it would make since we had located two banks of rams which we planned to stalk in the morning. With .22 shorts I knocked over a half-dozen big tender and trusting blues. We cut them up, floured them, fried them in deep fat. Never have I eaten a better meal. It put strength in my legs, ambition in my head, and next day my companion and I went up and got those two big rams. A little ability with a pistol or revolver comes in pretty handy at times.

I know of no type of shooting which lends itself any better to dry firing than the handgun. Anyone who wants to get good should do a lot of it. A miniature target on the wall of a room is all anyone needs. If he practices squeezing off dry shots at this for fifteen minutes a day, he'll be surprised at how much his scores will improve on the range.

23

The Handgun's a Barrel of Fun

MANY YEARS AGO a friend and I took a two-week trip for mule deer and turkey in the pine-clad mesa country of northern Arizona. In our optimism we toted along a couple of steaks for our first night in camp and a roast to cook in our Dutch oven. After that we figured to live off the country. Each carried a Springfield .30/06 sporter, carefully sighted in with a Lyman 48 receiver sight. On the unlikely chance that something might happen to one of the rifles, we carried a spare—a .30 Remington pump-action.

All of which was fine. But the deer and turkeys wouldn't cooperate. We saw fine birds almost every day, but always just as they were disappearing into the woods. And although we spotted does and fawns, we encountered no bucks. Presently we were reduced to a diet of beans, canned vegetables, and Dutch-oven bread. What put us back on a meat diet was a .22 caliber Colt Police Positive target revolver that I had tossed into my pack, along with four boxes of cartridges. Squirrels were plentiful that year, and the humble little .22 kept us from going meat-hungry. I was only a fair handgun shot, but my pal was really good, so we could get the makings of a squirrel stew anytime by hunting around camp for half an hour. They were so abundant that shooting them with a shotgun would have been murder and even knocking them off with a .22 rifle not much fun. But hunting them with a handgun was sport of a high order, since squirrels do not have the cover in Western yellow pines they have in the leafy hardwood trees of the East.

We hunted for ten days before either of us connected with anything larger than a squirrel—and then our luck changed astonishingly. I shot two turkeys with old full-metal-case 1917 military ammunition, and was lugging them back to camp when I heard the bellow of my companion's rifle about a mile away. He had killed a big buck. Later I too got a buck, and he collected a black bear and a turkey.

But if it hadn't been for the little .22 revolver, we probably could not have stayed in that excellent game country until our luck changed.

Along with a shotgun, a big-game rifle, and a varmint rifle of some sort, a good handgun belongs in the battery of every man interested in firearms and shooting. A handgun is a lot of fun to plink with, and skill acquired with it is quickly translated into skill with a rifle. Because of its light weight and small bulk it can be carried when a longer and heavier weapon would be left at home.

A pal of mine does a lot of trout fishing in a canyon that is infested with rattlesnakes, and in the course of years they have bitten several anglers. So a little .22 automatic with a 4 ½-inch barrel is an important part of his equipment. Each season he knocks the heads off from ten to twenty rattlers. Largely because of his efforts and those of a few other pistol-packin' fishermen, the snakes are being put under control.

A great advantage of the handgun is its small weight and bulk. It can be taken along when no one would think of lugging a rifle, and the handgun owner can get a lot of informal practice on occasions where otherwise he probably wouldn't shoot at all. For some years I spent a couple of weeks each summer with my family in an isolated cabin at 9,000-feet elevation in northern Arizona. My wife loves to fish for trout, and it was up to me to keep our young from slitting each other's throats while she did so. To pass the time, I kept on hand several hundred rounds of .22 Long Rifle and .38 Special ammunition, some targets, and a couple of handguns. And brother, the practice sharpened me up for rifle shooting.

The unique Thompson/Center Contender is a single-shot available as a rimfire or in about two dozen centerfire calibers, with interchangeable barrels. This one is mounted with a 1½X scope. In expert hands this pistol is a fine hunting arm.

Under certain conditions the handgun can be used on varmints. Years ago, big antelope jackrabbits were astonishingly plentiful in the Southwest—so plentiful and tame that shooting them with a rifle was no sport at all. I used to take a .22 revolver with me and pop away at jacks within 100-yard range. I missed a lot beyond 50 yards, of course, but I also hit enough to keep me interested.

Just what sort of handgun should this general-purpose job be? One thing's certain—it should be a .22, for which ammunition is cheap, widely distributed, and deadly on small game. Report and recoil are light, so the .22 is the one to learn with.

I'm often asked if .22 Shorts will seriously damage the chambers of a revolver. In the days before the introduction of noncorrosive priming, all .22 weapons had a relatively short life. That's because a high concentration of rust-causing priming salts in .22 cartridges quickly started oxidation in any arm chambered for them. If a revolver was used with Shorts, the forward portion of each chamber would pit; then it became difficult to seat the longer .22 Long Rifle cartridge. When the cartridge was fired, it was hard to extract the case, because its forward portion had expanded a trifle into the pits.

That particular headache hasn't existed for many years, because all .22 rimfire ammunition has been primed with various noncorrosive mixtures. Now the only hazard is erosion—eating away the steel of the chamber by hot powder gases. That's not much of a problem. Pressures are low in .22 ammunition. The amount of powder used is small, and burning is relatively cool. So, while theoretically the long-continued use of Shorts will eventually cause pitting and make it hard to seat .22 Long Rifle cartridges, actually that contingency is very remote. I have a Smith & Wesson K-22 through which I've shot thousands of rounds of Shorts, and thousands of Long Rifles as well. As far as I can tell, Long Rifle cartridges seat as easily as they ever did. And by using Shorts for plinking I have probably saved enough money to buy a couple of new cylinders.

A handgun for informal target shooting, plinking, and small-game hunting should, I believe, have a fairly short barrel. From 4 to 5 inches is about right, although many prefer longer barrels. The Ruger standard model has a 4³/₄-inch barrel; the Smith & Wesson .22 Combat Masterpiece and the

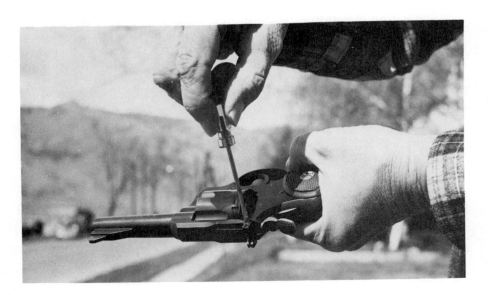

The hand gunner, when aiming, should pay more attention to his sights than the target. Here the "windage" is being adjusted on a target revolver.

S. & W. .22/32 Kit Gun have 4-inch barrels. The Colt Sport Model Woods-man and the Challenger have $4^1/_2$-inch barrels. A 6-inch barrel is not bad, though. I have used a Colt Officers' Model .22 and a Smith & Wesson K-22 for years. A pal of mine has shot hundreds of grouse and cottontails with a Harrington & Richardson Model 999, and a trapper I know has carried an Iver Johnson Model 833 Sealed 8 thousands of miles on a trapline, collecting hundreds of dollars' worth of spruce squirrels with it.

Anyone who will do much small-game shooting with a .22 handgun has a lot of suprises in store. I got one of the biggest shocks of my life when I discovered that three grouse out of four fly away when hit squarely through the body with a .22 high-speed solid-point bullet. The remedy is to use hollow-points. There may be some handgun men good enough to shoot the heads off grouse at from 15 to 30 yards, but I've never seen one do his stuff.

It seems strange that with solid bullets the .22 Short is apparently much more deadly on small game than is the .22 Long Rifle. I didn't believe that until I shot blue grouse for the pot now and then with a revolver. About three-fourths of those hit with Long Rifle solids flew away, and if it weren't for a very remarkable dog, I'd often have gone grouse-hungry.

A friend—a man who always carries a .22 handgun and who has killed hundreds of grouse with it—told me that I'd do better with .22 Shorts. He contended that the Long Rifle solid bullet goes clear through the grouse, wasting most of its energy, but that the Shorts stop inside the body and effect a kill. His own grouse pistol was a little Hi-Standard chambered for Shorts. I tried it and it bore out his argument, for I killed three-fourths of the grouse I hit.

There is a lot of fun to be had with the plinking handgun, but anyone who uses it should also use some judgment. The chap who gets bored with trout fishing and starts popping away at random in a spot where there are fifteen to twenty fishermen to the mile is making enemies for all handgun users. So is the lad who picnics in a farmer's wood lot and then leaves it littered with pop bottles he has broken with his .22 handgun. It's a grand and instructive little weapon if it's treated right and not abused.

24

Handgun Cartridges

THE CARTRIDGE that is the most widely shot in the United States is the familiar .22, and probably nine-tenths of all cartridges fired in handguns are these humble and inexpensive rimfires. Without having access to manufacturers' records, I'd likewise guess that about three-fourths of all handguns sold are chambered for the .22 rimfires.

Only two of the .22 rimfires are commonly used in handguns—the .22 Short and the .22 Long Rifle. In the past, however, some Colt and perhaps other revolvers were chambered for the odd-size .22 Winchester Special, or .22 W.R.F. When fired in a short-barreled handgun a .22 rimfire cartridge has some velocity loss, of course, but not as much as might be expected because, I understand, even the .22 Long Rifle high-velocity ammunition develops full velocity in about 18 inches of barrel.

Let's look at some figures:

According to the Western Ammunition Handbook, the .22 Short Super-X cartridge with its 29-grain bullet shows a muzzle velocity of 1,125 fps in a rifle, but when the same cartridge is fired in a handgun with a 6-inch barrel the velocity is 1,035, or a loss of about 100 fps. With the standard-velocity .22 Short in Xpert, the loss is likewise 100 fps, or 965 in a rifle and 865 in a handgun. In a .22 Long Rifle match load the velocity in a rifle is 1,145 and in a handgun 950—in this case a loss of about 200 fps. With the Super-X or high-velocity .22 Long Rifle cartridge fired in a rifle the velocity is 1,335 with the 40-grain bullet, but in a handgun 1,125. This greater velocity loss probably comes from the use of slower-burning powder.

At any event the .22 rimfire cartridge deserves its place as the overwhelming No. 1 handgun cartridge in popularity. It is cheap, accurate, pleasant to shoot, easy on the barrel. A .22 handgun is always the smartest buy for the beginner.

A revolver in .22 caliber can be used with .22 Short, Long, or Long Rifle cartridges. Long-continued use with .22 shorts will supposedly erode the forward part of the chamber and make the .22 Long Rifle cartridge difficult to insert and eject eventually. However, in these days of noncorrosive priming and the protective fouling left by waxed and greased bullets, it takes a long time and a lot of shooting to cause enough erosion to complicate things. In the meantime a revolver owner would probably save enough money by using .22 shorts to buy a new cylinder.

THE .25 CALIBER CENTERFIRES

The .25 Automatic is a small handgun cartridge which is still loaded but which will probably be discontinued someday. It was designed originally, I believe, for the little pocket pistol invented by John Browning and manufactured in the United States by Colt and in Europe by Fabrique Nationale and a great many other manufacturers. It isn't much of a cartridge as it uses a 50-grain bullet with a velocity of only 820 fps in the 2-inch barrel common to such pistols. Only one .25 caliber automatic pistol (the Sterling) is at present manufactured in the United States, and a few weapons of that caliber are imported from France, Belgium, and Spain.

THE FOREIGN .30S

Two interesting cartridges for which American pistols have never been made but which have sold fairly well in the United States are the .30 Mauser (or 7.63mm) and the .30 Luger (7.65). Both cartridges originated in Germany. The 7.63mm was designed for the big Mauser military pistol, which has a clip magazine forward of the trigger guard, which has an exotic look, and which is often equipped with a hollow wooden rifle-type buttstock that also serves as a scabbard. Pressures with his cartridge run high—about 30,000 pounds per square inch—and the velocity with the 86-grain bullet as loaded in the United States is 1,420! This is the same cartridge which is used in the Russian Tokarev service automatic, but it is doubtful if the Russians load it that hot.

The .30 Luger is used in the widely imported Luger pistol, which is also chambered for the 9mm Luger cartridge. With its 93-grain bullet at 1,250 in a 4½-inch barrel it is a pleasant cartridge to shoot. At one time before varmint rifles were as highly developed as they are now it was fashionable to purchase those 93-grain bullets and load them with enough powder to give high velocity into .30/06 cases.

THE .32 CALIBERS

Oddly enough all of the .32 caliber handgun cartridges are miserably misnamed. They are simply oversize .30s. The .32 Smith & Wesson has a bullet diameter of .315 inch, for instance, instead of the .308 of the standard .30. The .32 S. & W. is a standard cartridge for small pocket revolvers. It drives an 85-grain bullet at 720 fps in a 3-inch barrel and has a muzzle energy of only 98 feet-pounds. No powerhouse!

25 (6.35mm.)   32   32 Short   32 Colt   32–20 Win.   30 Luger   32 S. & W.   32 Long   32 (7.65mm.)
Auto. pistol   S. & W.   colt   new police   (7.65mm.)   long   colt   Auto. pistol
                                           Auto. pistol

The smaller centerfire handgun cartridges include, left to right, the .25 Automatic, the .32 Smith & Wesson, the .32 Short Colt, the .32 Colt New Police, the .32/20 Winchester, the .30 Luger (7.65mm), the .32 Smith & Wesson Long, the .32 Long Colt, and the .32 Auto Pistol (7.65mm).

Colt and Smith & Wesson revolvers (the .32 Hand Ejector and .32 Regulation Police in S. & W. brand and the Colt Courier, Detective Special, Cobra, and Police Positive in .32) are chambered for the .32 Smith & Wesson Long cartridge and will all accept the .32 S. & W., the .32 S. & W. Long, the .32 S. & W. Mid-Range, and the .32 Colt New Police ammunition. The .32 Short Colt cartridge is an old one and on its last legs. Its 80-grain bullet measures .313 and has a muzzle velocity of 800 fps in a 4-inch barrel. The .32 Long Colt, another old-timer, has identical ballistics.

The .32 W.C.F. or .32/20 cartridge is an entirely different animal. It is primarily a rifle cartridge, having been designed for the old Winchester Model 1873 rifle. It was also used in the stronger Model 92 Winchester and in various other rifles including Savage bolt-actions. In the standard-velocity form, it uses a 100-grain bullet at a velocity of 1,030 in a 6-inch barrel. Ammunition is loaded with lead, jacketed soft-point, and full-metal-cased bullets. In a rifle the ammunition has a velocity of 1290 fps. A cartridge for the revolver owner to avoid is the high-speed rifle cartridge that drives an 80-grain bullet at 2,180. It will shake a .32/20 revolver to pieces or even blow it up! For the power it always seemed to me that the .32/20 fired in a revolver had a lot of muzzle blast. Perhaps that is because the ammunition is loaded with relatively slow-burning powder.

The .32 Auto cartridge, or .32 Automatic Colt Pistol Cartridge (.32 A.C.P.), is another cartridge that was developed for the Browning pocket pistol made in the United States by Colt and in Belgium by F.N. It uses a bullet measuring .314 inch and weighing 71 grains at a velocity of 980 fps. Because of the governmental restrictions on small pocket pistols, Colt has ceased manufacture of the .32 Auto, but the cartridge still sells widely over the world. In Europe it is known as the 7.65mm. Browning and a vast array of handguns are made for it—Mauser pocket pistols (not the military), Frommer, Steyer, Peiper, Walther, Sauer, etc. In the United States, Savage,

| 380 (9mm.)
Aut. pistol | 38 S. & W. | 38 Short colt | 357
Magnum | 9mm. Luger
auto. pistol | 38 Auto.
colt pistol | 38 Special | 38 Colt
new police |

From left to right, the .380 Auto Pistol (9mm), .38 Smith & Wesson, .38 Short Colt, .357 Magnum, 9mm Luger Auto Pistol, .38 Auto Colt Pistol, .38 Special, and .38 Colt New Police.

Remington, Smith & Wesson, and Harrington & Richardson pistols have been made for it.

THE .38S

The so-called .38 revolver and pistol cartridges come a lot closer to being .35s. A widely used .38 is the cartridge known as the .38 Smith & Wesson and also as the .38 Colt New Police. It is generally loaded with a 145-grain bullet at a velocity of 745 fps. Bullet measures .359. The cartridge is widely used in Colt and Smith & Wesson revolvers and in the past other American revolvers have been chambered for it. The cartridge is just the same as the British .380 service cartridge, except that the British cartridge takes a 200-grain bullet at lower velocity. The .38 S. & W. cartridge will not chamber in a revolver made for the .38 Special cartridge.

The .38/40, on the other hand, employs a bullet that is larger than the other .38s. Whereas most of them run around .357, the .38/40 bullet measures .40 in. Like the .32/20 cartridge the .38/40 was designed for the old Winchester Model 1873 rifle and was likewise used in Model 1892 Winchesters chambered for it. The cartridge is dying but at one time Colt single-action Army and New Service revolvers were chambered for it.

The .38 Colt Automatic was designed for the Colt Military pistol. The 130-grain bullet measures .359 and has a velocity of 1,070 fps in the standard form for the older pistols and 1,300 in form of the .38 Super Auto for the Colt pistol of that name.

Another widely used .38 cartridge is the .380 Colt Auto, or, as it is known in Europe, the 9mm Browning Short or Kurz. Bullet measures .346 inch, weighs 95 grains, and leaves the muzzle at 970 fps. Cartridge is sort of a large-diameter .32 A.C.P. and was used in the now obsolete Colt pocket pistol as well as in Remington and Savage pocket pistols. In Europe it is very popular and a horde of automatic pistols made there are chambered for it. The famous 9mm Luger cartridge for Colt, Smith & Wesson, Luger, P-38, and other European automatic pistols drives a 115-grain bullet 1,150 fps.

THE .38 SPECIAL SERIES

The now-obsolete .38 Short Colt cartridge was designed for Colt police and pocket revolvers brought out in the 1880s and 1890s, such as the Double Action .38. As recently loaded it took a .357 bullet weighing 130 grains at a velocity of 770 fps. The .38 Long Colt is much more powerful and takes a 150-grain bullet at 785. It was at one time the U.S. Service cartridge in the .38 Army revolver, which eventually became the Official Police revolver. A revolver chambered for the .38 Long will shoot the .38 Short, just as one chambered for the .22 Long Rifle will shoot the .22 Short.

When the Americans were fighting in the Philippines, they found that an indignant Moro often could get within bolo range of an American soldier even if thoroughly perforated by .38 Long bullets. The army wanted a handgun cartridge with more authority and eventually the .45 Automatic (.45 A.C.P.) was adopted. In the meantime, however, Daniel Wesson, president of Smith & Wesson, had developed a more potent .38, the .38 Smith & Wesson Special, with a longer case, a heavier bullet, and more powder. It was not adopted by the army but it went on to become the most popular of all American centerfire revolver cartridges and probably the most accurate centerfire handgun cartridge in the world. Surely it is in this country the most reloaded, the most used, and the most widely sold. Standard load is a 158-grain bullet at a velocity of 870 in a 6-inch barrel, but it is made as a midrange wadcutter for target work with a 148-grain bullet at 770 and with a 200-grain bullet at 745, and in high-speed form with a 150-grain bullet at 1,100 fps. But this last should be used regularly only in heavy-frame revolvers. Revolvers chambered for the .38 Special will take cartridges in .38 Short and .38 Long caliber.

The famous .357 Magnum cartridge is a further refinement of the .38 Special with a still longer case—about $1/_{10}$ inch longer than the .38 Special, and .38 Short, Long, and .38 Special cartridges will chamber and fire in a .357. The .357 Magnum drives a 158-grain bullet at 1,450 fps in an $8^3/_8$-inch barrel. Pressures are in the rifle class and the recoil is formidable. Colt, Smith & Wesson, and Ruger make revolvers for it.

THE .44S

The .44 Smith & Wesson American cartridge, which is now obsolete, bears the same relationship to the .44 Smith & Wesson Russian as the .38 Short Colt bears to the .38 Long, and the Long, in turn, bears the same relationship to the .44 S. & W. Special as the .38 Long does to the .38 Special.

The ancient .44 Smith & Wesson American was made for the old .44 American army revolver, which was introduced to the service about 1871. Like the .44 Colt, the .44 Webley, and the .44 Bulldog, it is no longer made.

The .44 Smith & Wesson Russian is still loaded, however, with a .431-inch bullet weighing 246 grains at a velocity of 770 fps in a 6 $1/_2$-inch barrel. In its day it was a red-hot target cartridge. It was originally designed by Smith & Wesson for the Russian army revolver which was at one time standard with the old Imperial Russian army. The .44 Russian led to the development of the .44 S. & W. Special, and uses the same bullets with

Some of the big handgun cartridges: From left to right, the .44 Remington Magnum, the .44 Smith & Wesson Special, the .45 Colt, the .45 Auto, and the .45 Auto Rim.

44 Remington mag.   44 S. & W. Special   45 Colt   45 Auto.   45 Auto. rim.

more powder and more velocity. At the present the two cartridges are factory-loaded to the same velocity, but for the Special this is a decided underload. Almost all .44 Special owners are handloaders, and, led by Elmer Keith, the Salmon, Idaho, gun writer and handgun expert, they developed some right hot loads for the Specials. One famous one is the 250-grain Keith bullet in front of 18.5 grains of No. 2400 for a velocity of 1,200 fps. I have shot it in my own .44 Special and it is a mean combination, both fore and aft!

It was loads like that that led to the development of the world's most powerful handgun cartridge, the .44 Smith & Wesson Magnum. The beautiful, wonderful, and fearful revolver for this tremendous cartridge is a veritable hand rifle, as the 240-grain bullet is driven at 1,570 fps at the muzzle by a charge of 22 grains of what looks like No. 2400 but may or may not be. It is three times as powerful as the old .45 Colt and almost twice as powerful as the famous .357 Magnum. And incidentally, the .357 Magnum, the .41 Magnum, and the .44 Magnum are the only three new American centerfire cartridges that have appeared in a whole flock of blue moons.

The .44/40 cartridge is not a .44, but about a .42, since the bullet measures .426 in. It was developed for the old Winchester Model 73 rifles, and is hence a rifle cartridge, but it was much used and liked in the old West when people could use the same ammunition in both their Winchester rifles and their Colt Frontier revolvers.

THE .45S

An old Winchester catalog published before World War I lists the .45 Webley, the .45 Colt, and the .45 Smith & Wesson; but now only two .45 caliber handgun cartridges are loaded in this country. One is the .45 Colt for which the Model 1873 single-action Army revolver was chambered and for which the Colt New Service was adapted. It pushes a 255-grain bullet along at 870 fps from a 5 1/2-inch barrel. The cartridge is still alive and well liked and the revived Colt single-action is made for it.

The other .45 on the lists is, of course, the .45 Automatic in its various loadings, generally using 230-grain bullets at velocities ranging from 750 to 870 fps. It is used in the Model 1911 Colt automatic which is the standard of the U.S. army.

Index